STALKING
BILLY THE KID

MARC SIMMONS BOOKS FROM SUNSTONE PRESS:

Yesterday in Santa Fe (1989)
Turquoise and Six-Guns (2000)
New Mexico Mavericks (2005)
Stalking Billy the Kid (2006)

OTHER PUBLISHED WORKS:

Witchcraft in the Southwest (1974)
Coronado's Land (1991)
The Last Conquistador, Juan de Oñate (1991)
Massacre on the Lordsburg Road (1997)
Following the Santa Fe Trail, A Guide (2001)
Spanish Pathways (2001)
Kit Carson & His Three Wives (2003)

STALKING BILLY THE KID

Brief Sketches of a Short Life

Marc Simmons

SANTA FE

Cover Art, Map and Illustrations on page 81 and 109 by Ron Kil.
All photographs and illustrations are from the author's
collection unless otherwise indicated.

The introduction, "Billy the Kid and the Lincoln County War," was first published in *American History Illustrated*, vol. XVII, no. 4, June 1982, pp. 40-44, and appears courtesy of Primedia History Group, 741 Miller Drive SE, Suite C1, Leesburg, VA.

Book design by Vicki Ahl

© 2006 by Marc Simmons. All rights reserved.

No part of this book may be reproduced in any form or by any electronic or mechanical means including information storage and retrieval systems without permission in writing from the publisher, except by a reviewer who may quote brief passages in a review.

Sunstone books may be purchased for educational, business, or sales promotional use. For information please write: Special Markets Department, Sunstone Press, P.O. Box 2321, Santa Fe, New Mexico 87504-2321.

Library of Congress Cataloging-in-Publication Data:
Simmons, Marc.
 Stalking Billy the Kid : brief sketches of a short life / Marc Simmons.
   p. cm.
 Includes bibliographical references.
 ISBN 0-86534-525-2 (softcover : alk. paper)
 1. Billy, the Kid–Anecdotes. 2. Outlaws–Southwest, New–Biography–Anecdotes.
3. Southwest, New–Biography–Anecdotes. 4. Frontier and pioneer life–Southwest, New–Anecdotes. I. Title.

F786.B54S56 2006
364.15'52092–dc22
[B]
                                          2006015282

WWW.SUNSTONEPRESS.COM
SUNSTONE PRESS / POST OFFICE BOX 2321 / SANTA FE, NM 87504-2321 /USA
(505) 988-4418 / ORDERS ONLY (800) 243-5644 / FAX (505) 988-1025

FOR MY FRIEND

Phyllis S. Morgan
who can get things done

CONTENTS

PREFACE / 11
INTRODUCTION: Billy The Kid and the Lincoln County War / 17
1 / AN OUTLAW'S BOYHOOD / 35
2 / BILLY THE KID'S MOTHER / 41
3 / A FIRST JAIL BREAK / 46
4 / THE LOST YEARS OF BILLY THE KID / 49
5 / DOBIE AND THE KID / 55
6 / A TUNSTALL DOCUMENT / 61
7 / BLAZING GUNS IN LINCOLN / 66
8 / A SUSAN WALLACE LETTER / 71
9 / ELFEGO AND THE KID IN ALBUQUERQUE / 76
10 / THE STRANGER WORE TWO GUNS / 82
11 / SUSAN MCSWEEN / 87
12 / SHARING A MEAL WITH BILLY THE KID / 93
13 / THE KILLING OF JUAN PATRÓN / 98
14 / THE GOVERNOR AND THE KID / 104
15 / PAT GARRETT'S BOOK / 111
16 / AN ENGLISHMAN MEETS BILLY / 117
17 / SOME BILLY THE KID IMPOSTERS / 123
18 / DID JESSE JAMES MEET BILLY THE KID? / 129
19 / A GRAVE QUESTION: WHERE IS BILLY BURIED? / 137
MAP OF FORT SUMNER / 172
APPENDIX 1 / "SETTLERS REJOICE" / 173
APPENDIX 2 / "THE BIVOUAC OF THE DEAD, 1882" / 175
APPENDIX 3 / PATHFINDER, IN SEARCH OF BILLY THE KID / 176
APPENDIX 4 / "BILLY QUOTES" / 180
NOTES / 186
SELECTED READINGS / 188
ABOUT THE AUTHOR / 193
ABOUT THE ILLUSTRATOR / 194

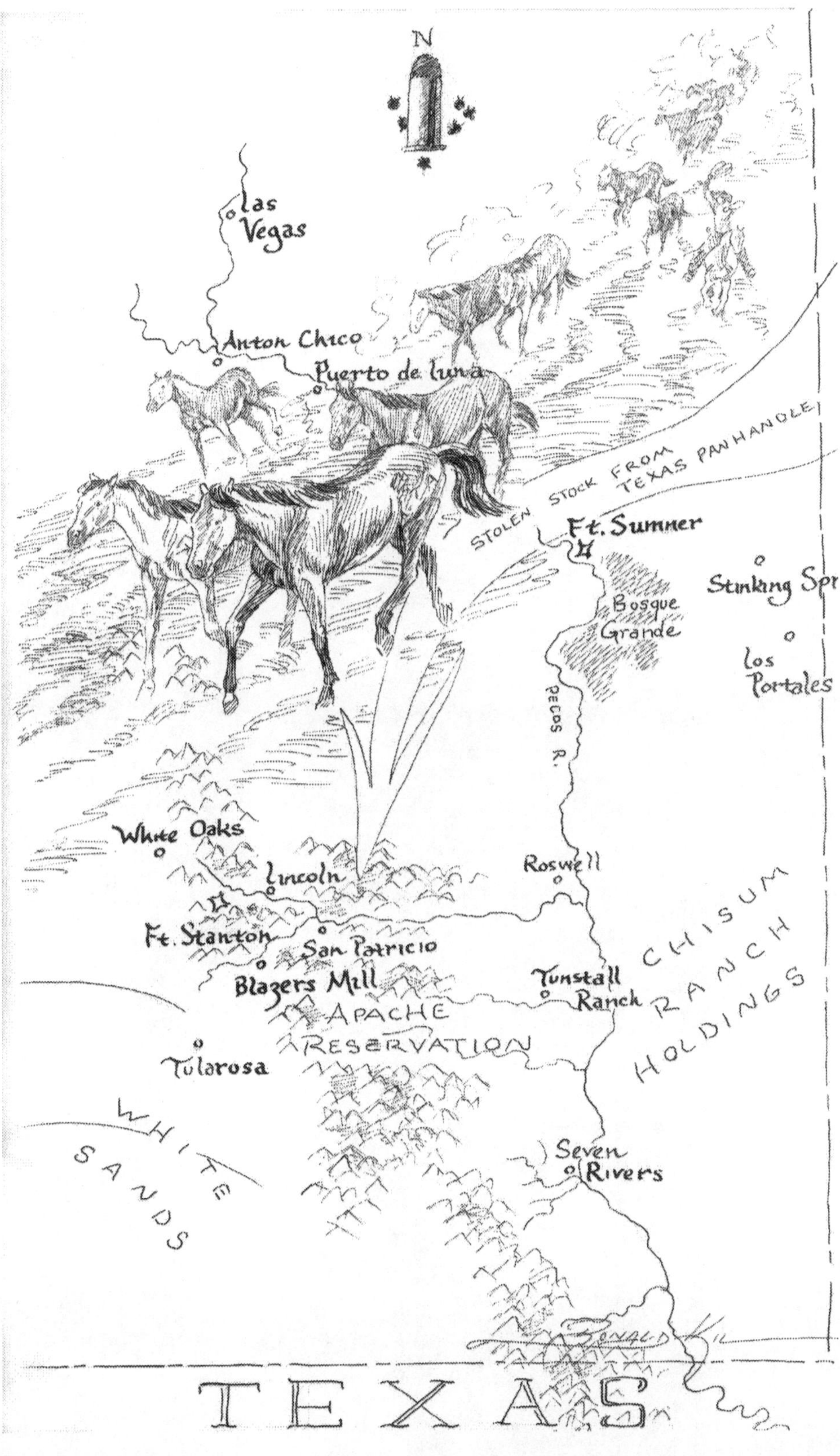

N

Las Vegas

Anton Chico

Puerto de Luna

STOLEN STOCK FROM TEXAS PANHANDLE

Ft. Sumner

Bosque Grande

Stinking Spr

Los Portales

PECOS R.

White Oaks

Lincoln

Roswell

Ft. Stanton

San Patricio

Blazers Mill

Tunstall Ranch

CHISUM RANCH HOLDINGS

APACHE RESERVATION

Tularosa

WHITE SANDS

Seven Rivers

TEXAS

PREFACE

Outlaws and gunfighters! They represent some of the most colorful and exciting figures who inhabited the Wild West. Our fascination with their violent and often abridged lives can be traced to a public fondness for unusual, dramatic, and eye-opening stories. Invariably, the careers of frontier desperadoes read like a western soap opera turned out by Hollywood script writers.

New Mexico in the days of the Territory had its fair share of hard-bitten men who rode sideways of the law. It became a "catch basin for rogues" in the vivid phrasing of Governor Miguel Otero. According to him, outlaws on the run from Texas, the Indian Territory, Colorado, and Arizona crossed the line into the wilds of New Mexico where they found a safe haven. The tales of their evil and bloody doings furnish a stirring chapter in the modern history of the state.

All summary accounts of New Mexico badmen must begin with William Bonney, alias Billy the Kid. Unquestionably, he was the West's most famous outlaw. For such a short life, much of it spent in a backwater territory, the Kid made quite a splash. No other New Mexican is better known world wide than he, even though at first glance his fame would seem to rest upon nothing more than a string of criminal acts.

At the time of his death in 1881, the twenty-one year old Billy had many friends among the local Hispanic population, as well as female admirers who found him romantic and charming. In some precincts, he was spoken of as a boy Robin Hood who stole from the wealthy and shared his spoils with the poor, although that depiction of him had more basis in myth than reality. Nevertheless, upon news of his death by the gun, newspapers throughout the nation seemed to agree with the sentiments expressed editorially in the *Grant County Herald* of Silver City (July 23, 1881): "The vulgar murderer and desperado known as Billy the Kid has met his just desserts at last."

It has been said that the verifiable facts about Billy the Kid's career are so thin that they scarcely fill a few pages. His biographer Robert M. Utley expressed it this way: "The Kid most people know is a product of this process [of mythmaking], a folk hero encrusted with so many layers of legend as to defy historical inquiry." That notwithstanding, numerous writers over the past century have accepted the challenge, churning out books and articles innumerable with the full expectation that each and all will find a readership, so beguiling is the name and life of this mercurial and forever youthful figure in frontier history.

Over more than a half century of my trafficking in Southwest history, I have been privileged to meet many of the authors and historians who have dealt with Billy the Kid and his story. The list includes Ramon F. Adams, Joel Jacobsen, Donald R. Lavash, J. Frank Dobie, Robert M. Utley, John P. Wilson, William Keleher, Howard Bryan, Leon Metz, and C.L. Sonnichsen.

One thing I learned from them was that you cannot write about the Kid and remain neutral. It seems one has to accept him either as a murdering little punk with no redeeming qualities, or as simply a misguided young man who was driven to a life of crime by chance and circumstance. There is scarcely any middle ground.

One man who attempted to find some was Governor Otero. He had been personally acquainted with Billy. In his memoirs published in 1936, Otero stated that Billy the Kid "I can honestly say was a man more sinned against than sinning."

Yet it remains difficult to define with precision the magnetic qualities possessed by the Kid that continue to attract a devoted following. Among the oddest of their number was Bonnie Parker who with her confederate and lover Clyde Barrow robbed banks in the Southwest during the 1930s. When both died, ambushed by lawmen on May 23, 1934 in eastern Louisiana, a single book was discovered in their bullet-riddled car, Walter Noble Burns, *The Saga of Billy the Kid*. It is on display today in the Depot Museum at Arcadia, Louisiana. The binding has disintegrated and the worn pages are held together by a ribbon.

Folk historian Don Dorais tells me that he believes Bonnie rather than Clyde was reader of the book, and that under its influence she may have seen in their crime spree parallels with some of Billy's activities. Indeed, he thinks Bonnie Parker may have consciously copied his lawless career path, having succumbed to the Kid's glamour-image.

Since I have written about New Mexico history for more than forty years, it was perhaps inevitable that now and then I should publish articles on Billy the Kid. Thus upon request, I was able to assemble here a collection of my varied writings pertaining to some of Billy's real or imagined deeds. Each piece that follows in this book opens a small window on an aspect of his tumultuous life, or casts light upon others whose fortunes intersected with his.

In this writing, I have stalked Billy in an erratic rather than a systematic way, taking pleasure merely in adding a few new and unusual fragments to his biography. I trust that readers who have a fascination with the history and legend of Billy the Kid will find in these pages something of interest and value. As Eugene Cunningham wrote more than seventy years ago: "In our imagination the Kid still lives—the Kid still rides."

For specific help I received in putting *Stalking Billy the Kid* together, I wish to thank Harry C. Myers, Mike Pitel, Cheryl and John P. Wilson, Bill Allen, Don Sweet, Lynda Sanchez, Robert "Doc" Sproull, Jan Girand, Maryln Bowlin and Mark L. Gardner.

Any errors that may be found in the text are entirely my responsibility.

—Marc Simmons
Cerrillos, New Mexico

Artist's image of Billy the Kid based on an original tintype. (New Mexico Department of Development)

INTRODUCTION

Billy the Kid and the Lincoln County War

"Every calculation based on experience elsewhere fails in New Mexico." So spoke Lew Wallace, once the youngest major general in the Union army, author of *Ben Hur,* and governor of New Mexico Territory at the height of the Lincoln County War.

Wallace's remark was not idly made, for during his three year governorship at Santa Fe, 1878–1881, he discovered to his dismay that the rules of politics and the rule of law, as he knew them in the East, did not apply there. Crooked lawyers, devious land speculators, claim jumpers, and cattle rustlers were as common as thorns on a cactus. And even many territorial officials and prominent business leaders engaged openly in corruption, on the theory, it would appear, that in this turbulent land, honest men were prime candidates for the poorhouse.

Governor Samuel B. Axtell, Wallace's immediate predecessor, for example, had been removed from office after his administration was linked to frauds, mismanagement, underhanded plots, and murders. He was a member of the notorious Santa Fe Ring, a group that controlled much of the Territory's economy and political life. Both Axtell and the Ring played an unsavory role behind the scenes in the Lincoln County War, leading President Rutherford B. Hayes to appoint Lew Wallace as house-cleaner and peacemaker.

Lincoln County, the focus of Wallace's attention during his term of office, had been carved out of the remote southeastern corner of the Territory in 1869. Stretching from the Texas line westward to the San Andres Mountains, it comprised more land than several New England states combined and, in fact, was the largest county in the nation.

Its sparse population was thinly scattered around the fringes of the arid Tularosa Basin, through a half dozen mountain ranges, and along the valley of the middle Pecos River. Some of its people were Hispanic farmers, originally from older settlements on the Rio Grande. A sprinkling of Texans owned ranches, large and small, down the east side. And there was an uncounted host of drifters, many of them on the run from the law and looking for a place to hide. By the mid 1870s, Lincoln County was already famous as an outlaw haven.

But there were other men who sought out this far country because in its untapped resources they perceived opportunities for economic development and personal profit. As was true elsewhere in New Mexico, achievement of those goals required gathering and holding the reins of political power. The Lincoln County War was a naked struggle for power unlike more traditional conflicts in the West born of personal feuds or rivalries between cattlemen, sheep raisers, and homesteaders. And behind it all lay the sinister and, to this day, shadowy hand of the Santa Fe Ring.

Among the early opportunists was a trio of Irishmen: Lawrence G. Murphy, James J. Dolan, and John H. Riley, operators of the only mercantile business in the county seat of Lincoln. Their "Big Store" monopolized trade in the area, charged farmers and ranchers exorbitant prices, and held beef contracts for the supply of neighboring Fort Stanton and the Mescalero Apache Reservation.

Murphy and his partners maintained close ties

with the Ring, depending upon its patronage and influence to win government contracts. They had the ear of Governor Axtell. Lincoln County Sheriff William Brady was their willing tool. For a time the tight mercantile monopoly, so carefully structured, seemed unassailable.

Allied against the proprietors of the Big Store, however, were three able men looking to enhance their own fortunes. One was John S. Chisum, who had driven a cattle herd out of Texas in 1873 and founded a ranch of king-size proportions on the Pecos near modern Roswell. Rustlers over a two year period stole 10,000 head of his stock, and he believed many of the animals had been purchased by Murphy's firm at Lincoln to fill beef contracts.

The second man, a friend of Chisum's, was Alexander McSween. A recently arrived Kansas lawyer, he had a hunger for political office and power. Basically honest, he looked with alarm upon the shoddy, often illegal, business practices of the Murphy-Dolan-Riley interests.

The third member of the group was a likable and ambitious Englishman in his early twenties, John Henry Tunstall. Funded by his father in London, he had come to Lincoln County determined to create a ranching empire. Establishing his headquarters on the Rio Feliz southeast of the county seat, he quickly discovered that the Big Store had local commerce and politics securely under its control.

McSween and Tunstall, finding that they had common aims, joined forces and opened a bank and a rival store in Lincoln. Much of their financial backing came from the pocket of John Chisum. By breaking the monopoly and undercutting prices, the new company was an overnight success.

About that time, Murphy went into semi-retirement because of ill health, leaving James Dolan to deal with the situation. Long-abused customers were abandoning the Big Store in droves and going over to the opposition. By fair means or foul, Dolan decided the competition had to be destroyed.

Into this charged atmosphere rode a young man, handy with a gun, who identified himself as William H. Bonney. In the less than four years of life remaining to him, this youthful desperado would shoot his way into the history books under the name Billy the Kid.

By all accounts, he scarcely looked the part of a killer. Under five feet, eight inches tall, Billy was slender and sinewy with noticeably small feet and hands.

Even after he had turned twenty, folks who knew him declared that he could pass for a sixteen-year-old.

The beardless Kid had a pointed chin and a short upper lip which exposed protruding front teeth and gave him a chronic grin. Women, if credence can be given to numerous reports, found him attractive.

Less unanimous are contemporary statements regarding his disposition. His legion of enemies delighted in picturing him as reckless and cruel with an inborn instinct for murder. From that view of Billy's character sprang the often-repeated claims that he shot his first victim at age twelve—a rogue who insulted his mother—and that by the time he died at twenty-one, he had slain a man for every year of his life. Both assertions were false.

Friends and partisans, on the other hand, testified that the Kid was easy-going, jocular in manner, loyal, and kindly disposed toward those giving him half a chance. But, they were quick to admit he was a remorseless and dangerous enemy. Some of the men who opposed him discovered that when they fell before his six-gun.

By the historical record, six killings, not twenty-one, can be credited definitely to the Kid. He appears to have had a hand in three others, during gunfights when lead flew in all directions. But even those, proclaimed his supporters, occurred because evil men backed him into a corner. The ongoing argument over Billy's motives and deeds forms but one of the many elements that cast a mythical glow over his personal history.

Controversy surrounds almost every aspect of his career, including even the place and date of his birth, which unsubstantiated reports place in New York City, November 23, 1859. The first valid reference to the youth does not surface until March 1, 1873. On that date records show that the widow Catherine McCarty married William H. Antrim in Santa Fe with her two young sons, Joseph and Henry McCarty, as witnesses. Henry, the future Billy the Kid, was then fourteen years old, and though high-spirited gave no other indication of the turbulent life that would be his.

The Antrims soon moved to Silver City, and the following year Catherine died of tuberculosis, leaving her sons adrift. Without her steadying hand, little Henry was soon at odds with the law. When a companion stole a bundle of clothes from two Chinamen, he was accused of the theft and lodged in the Silver City jail. Escaping by climbing up a chimney, he headed for the Arizona line—now and to the end of his days, a fugitive.

During the next two years, Henry Antrim (he had taken his stepfather's surname) worked quietly in southeastern Arizona as cowboy, farmhand, and teamster. Then, during the summer of 1877, he shot to death blacksmith Frank Cahill, who had been bullying him in a saloon near Camp Grant.

A coroner's jury ruled that the slaying "was criminal and unjustifiable, and that Henry Antrim, alias Kid, is guilty thereof." Had the young man's plea of self-defense been sustained, giving the verdict in his favor, much of what followed might have been avoided.

Jailed once more, the Kid escaped again and rode hard for New Mexico. After a brief stopover at Mesilla, on the Rio Grande forty miles above El Paso, he set a course for Lincoln County. Crossing the Guadalupe Mountains, where Apaches stole his horse, he descended to the Pecos Valley, arriving there footsore and hungry during the fall of 1877.

A hospitable ranching family gave him grub and a new mount. Moving upriver, he stayed briefly with the Chisum outfit. After several weeks he traveled west and landed at Tunstall's ranch. The foreman,

Richard Brewer, offered him a job.

Using the alias William H. Bonney to cloak his identity, the Kid enjoyed several months of calm, herding cattle. Quickly he came to admire his boss, John Henry Tunstall, who was just a few years his senior. And the liking was reciprocated. Of Billy, Tunstall remarked to an acquaintance, "That's the finest lad I ever met. I'm going to make a man out of that boy yet. He has it in him."

The Kid's sense of loyalty toward this man explains much about his conduct in the terrible sequence of events that soon unfolded.

James Dolan now was moving swiftly to counter the threat posed by the McSween-Tunstall firm in Lincoln. By illegal means, he obtained a writ of attachment on all their properties. His ally, Sheriff Brady, agreed to send a deputy with a large posse to Tunstall's ranch to serve the writ.

When word of the maneuver reached the Rio Feliz, young Tunstall decided to go to Lincoln and try to negotiate a settlement. Some evidence suggests that the Kid, fearing treachery, pleaded with his boss to take to the hills. Tunstall refused, and gathering several of his cowboys, including Brewer and Billy, he set out for the county seat.

On the way the posse came up and the hapless Englishman was shot in the back of the head. He had made no hostile move. It was a simple case of murder.

This crime proved to be the spark touching off the conflagration which became the Lincoln County War. Death of the popular rancher-merchant aroused indignation among county residents and led his employees and friends to swear vengeance. None was more determined in that regard than Billy the Kid.

Knowing that agencies of the law were firmly under the thumb of Dolan and his associates, Tunstall's men formed a body of "Regulators," commanded by Dick Brewer, to track down members of the killer posse. Two of them were captured in March and while being taken to Lincoln were "shot trying to escape," as the popular saying went.

Governor Axtell meanwhile was being subjected to severe criticism for his seeming indifference to the spreading trouble in the southern part of the Territory. Finally he did go to Lincoln and, accompanied by Dolan, who guided his every step, he conducted a perfunctory and wholly biased investigation. As a result, he issued a proclamation authorizing the commander at Fort Stanton to assist civil law officers in keeping the peace. That meant simply that Sheriff Brady, when in need, could call out the troops to defend the Dolan faction.

The bloodshed continued to escalate. On April 1, Billy and five other Regulators slipped into Lincoln intending to serve as bodyguards for the wives and children of McSween partisans. Sheriff Brady and several deputies were seen walking down the town's one street toward the courthouse. The opportunity was too good to be missed.

From behind a plank gate, Billy and his companions opened fire. Brady and George Hindman were immediately killed. The remaining deputies shot back, and the Kid received a minor flesh wound. Concealed by friends until nightfall, he stole away and rejoined the Regulators.

The slaying of Sheriff Brady proved a major blunder. It turned public opinion against Billy's crowd and discredited their cause. Blame for the killing was also heaped upon McSween, who had nothing to do with it. Recalled one resident years afterward, "Brady ... probably had faults but none that justified his being shot down like a dog."

The territorial press howled that anarchy reigned in Lincoln County. And so it seemed. A few days after the sheriff's death, the Regulators cornered "Buckshot" Roberts, another member of the posse that had killed Tunstall. At Blazer's Mill southwest of Lincoln, Roberts fought gamely and before he fell, shot Dick Brewer between the eyes.

Frank MacNab succeeded Brewer as head of the Regulators, but he died in a gunfight toward the end of April and leadership passed to "Doc" Scurlock. Ranging unchecked through the countryside, the Regulators gained the upper hand. The Dolan faction became frantic. Only the timely intervention of the Santa Fe Ring prevented its defeat.

In the capital, Thomas B. Catron, a leading Ringite, prevailed upon Governor Axtell to appoint George W. Peppin as the new sheriff of Lincoln County. Peppin, a pro-Dolan man, had been one of the deputies escaping the ambush that killed Brady. He was fully prepared to smite the enemy with fire and sword.

With this appointment, the stage was set for a showdown, and it was not long in coming. Between July 15 and 19, 1878, occurred "The Five Days Battle," the culmination of the Lincoln County War. Dolan had assembled his "troops" and under the generalship of Sheriff Peppin besieged McSween and fourteen followers in his Lincoln home.

During the affray Colonel Nathan Dudley, commander at Fort Stanton, arrived with soldiers and several pieces of artillery. But instead of intervening to end hostilities, he stood calmly by while the Peppin forces concluded the siege. The colonel's behavior can be traced to his friendliness toward Dolan and the Santa Fe Ring.

On the last day, the attackers set fire to McSween's house. Flames moved slowly through the adobe building, burning the plank floor and ceiling. Mrs. McSween left the smoking structure to plead with Colonel Dudley to spare the lives of her husband and the others. He declined.

The defenders retreated from room to room. With McSween exhausted and near collapse, Billy the Kid took charge. By dark, fire had forced them into the last room. The Kid ordered that, in turn, each man should make a wild dash for freedom. He managed to flee unscathed through the hail of lead, but Alexander McSween and four others died. In a blaze of gunfire, the war was virtually ended.

That was not entirely apparent at the time, however. Sporadic violence continued, but with both McSween and Tunstall gone, the Regulators as a group disintegrated. Shocked by reports of the Five Days

Battle, President Hayes removed Governor Axtell from office and on September 30 replaced him with Lew Wallace. Also spurring him to take this action had been remonstrances from the British Foreign Officer over the killing of Tunstall.

Committed to bring order out of chaos, the new governor found the issues surrounding the war almost too perplexing to unravel. Since he was confused over who were the injured parties, he proclaimed a general amnesty for all participants. But it did not cover those who might be convicted of slaying Sheriff Brady.

Murphy died while convalescing at Santa Fe. Dolan lost his store to mortgage foreclosure, while his junior partner, Riley, left the county. Colonel Dudley, condemned for his actions during the burning of the McSween house, was relieved of his post at Fort Stanton. In January 1880 Governor Wallace was pleased to report to the territorial legislature that peace had been restored in Lincoln County.

Yet one untidy piece of business remained outstanding. Billy the Kid was still at large. With a remnant of the Regulators, he had formed an outlaw gang and turned to rustling. That played straight into the hands of the Santa Fe Ring. Since things had gone awry in Lincoln County, the Ringites made the Kid their scapegoat. The Santa Fe *New Mexican*, a mouthpiece for the group, took the lead in laying blame for old troubles and every new crime in the Territory squarely upon the shoulders of William Bonney.

In late 1880 a tall, gangling man with a walrus mustache assumed duties as the sheriff of Lincoln County. Pat Garrett had been living in the Pecos Valley around Fort Sumner and Roswell but played no part in the just-concluded war. His assignment as a lawman was to track down Billy the Kid. A standing reward of $500 for the desperado, offered by Governor Wallace, provided Garrett added incentive.

On December 21 the sheriff captured Billy and three accomplices at Stinking Springs, an abandoned cow camp twenty-five miles east of Fort Sumner. After a brief period of imprisonment in Santa Fe, the outlaw was sent by rail down to Mesilla to stand trial for the murder of Sheriff Brady.

The long arm of the Ring, reaching into the courtroom, sealed the Kid's fate. Although it could not be proved that he had shot Brady, his mere presence among the assailants, declared the judge, was sufficient for a guilty verdict. The handpicked jury readily complied, and the defendant was ordered returned to Lincoln for execution.

Pat Garrett in his later years. (After E. Hough)

Back once more in the little town that figured so prominently in his life, Billy the Kid sat on the second floor of the courthouse to await the gallows. From his window, he could see the blackened ruins of the McSween residence.

On April 27, 1881 Pat Garrett departed Lincoln for the town of White Oaks to purchase lumber for the scaffold. In his absence Billy obtained a gun, hidden in the privy by a friend. Killing the two deputies left to guard him, he mounted a horse and rode out of Lincoln for the last time.

His dramatic escape threw the Territory into an uproar. Garrett, much chagrined by the turn of events, formed a posse and took up the chase.

Why the Kid did not turn immediately toward Mexico will always remain a mystery. Instead, he rode northward to Fort Sumner, counting on friends to take him in. There Pat Garrett surprised him in a darkened room of the Pete Maxwell house on the night of July 14. The sheriff fired two shots and Billy the Kid fell dead.

While his foes breathed a sigh of relief, there were many, counting themselves as his friends, who mourned.

Bitter memories of the Lincoln County War persisted far into the 20th century. It is today ranked as one of the most lawless episodes in the history of the American West.

Thought to be an image of Billy the Kid in his Silver City years (unproven).

1

AN OUTLAW'S BOYHOOD

Someone once handed me a newspaper clipping from the old *New York World*, dated July 26, 1881. It was a story about Billy the Kid, who had been killed at Fort Sumner, New Mex. just the week before.

According to the clipping, the Kid, alias William Bonney, was really "Michael McCarthy and he was born on Vanderwater Street in New York City." It was further stated that the youth had fled after killing Thomas Moore, a brushmaker, at the corner of Pearl and Hague streets, September 9, 1876.

To back up its story, the *World* cited a local detective who had gone out West, to New Mexico, on business. There he had met the outlaw shortly before his death, and Billy had admitted that he was originally from New York.

This newspaper account, however, is quite garbled, as are most of the early-day reports about the Kid's beginnings. Biographer Robert M. Utley says that "his origins are shrouded in mystery and buffeted by controversy."

The *World* acknowledged as much. In the second part of its story, it gave a different version, one that disputed Billy's having murdered a brushmaker in Manhattan and gone on the lamb.

This second tale had been secured just the day before by a reporter who interviewed a visitor to New York City, Mr. Charles H. Gildersleeve. He was a prominent lawyer and member of the territorial legislature from Santa Fe. (Today, his name is on a city street in the New Mexico capital.)

Mr. Gildersleeve asserted that he knew Billy the Kid very well by sight, having frequently seen him in the Santa Fe jail. And he professed to be familiar with the famous desperado's past history.

The lawyer said that the Kid was brought up in New Mexico at a stage station kept by his mother, who had married a soldier 15 years ago. In Gildersleeve's words, "The stage station, a cross between a tavern and a saloon, was the place where Billy received his education, and he was always considered a bad boy."

In reality, these claims were pure poppycock. The Kid's mom never had a station, nor did she marry a soldier. Politician Gildersleeve must have wanted to see his name in the papers, so he fabricated a yarn.

The first definite record of the Kid comes from Santa Fe, March 1, 1873. On that date, Henry McCarty (his real name, not Michael McCarthy, as the *World* had it) stood as witness in the second marriage of his mother, Catherine McCarty, to William Antrim at the First Presbyterian Church.

The Kid then would have been in his early teens. So where was he actually born and in what place did he grow up?

Utley believes that Catherine and her first husband immigrated from Ireland during the great potato famine and settled in New York. There in the Irish slums of Manhattan or Brooklyn, Henry McCarty was born. (He would later take the name Billy, after his step-father William Antrim.) His birth year seems to have been 1859 or 1860.

After loss of her husband, Catherine went to Indianapolis, where she met Antrim, and by 1870 they moved to Wichita, Kans. When she developed tuberculosis, another move was made to New Mexico, to take advantage of the healthful climate.

Following a short stay at Santa Fe, to formally tie the knot, the Antrims took up residence in Silver City. It was there that Billy started getting into trouble, a course that would eventually lead him into the thick of the Lincoln County War.

From the start of the Silver City phase of his life, the Kid's personal history is fairly well documented. But you would never guess that in reading the final paragraphs of the *New York World's* story. It is loaded with nonsense.

Here is a couple of samples: "Billy the Kid has killed 15 men in cold blood, some of them on the most trivial pretext. He claims to have killed a man for every year of his life."

In fact, the Kid is thought to have killed a total of only six men. Justified or not, he believed that in every case he had plenty of admissible cause.

"Billy had a band of freebooters and assassins under his control," said the *World*, "and it was composed of the most desperate men. Farmers and ranchers within a radius of 100 miles were kept in complete subjection and lived in a state of terror."

Some of the Kid's enemies, indeed, made that claim. But he also had many friends in the countryside who sheltered and protected him.

The old newspaper stories seldom furnish reliable history, but at this late date they make interesting and exciting reading.

The Antrim home in Silver City where Billy spent his early teens.

2

BILLY THE KID'S MOTHER

In 1975 the Silver City Garden Club sent a petition to Santa Fe asking that an official state highway historical sign be posted at the entrance of their local pioneer cemetery. Among the prominent people buried there were city founder John Bullard, famous lion and bear hunter Ben Lilly, and Mrs. Catherine Antrim, mother of Billy the Kid.

The matter was referred to the State Cultural Properties Review Committee for approval The two historian members were the state archivist Dr. Myra Ellen Jenkins and myself.

I knew that Dr. Jenkins had a particular aversion to Billy the Kid, so I was not surprised when she vigorously opposed granting the Garden Club's request.

To me her objections seemed trivial, so I made a rather heated defense for the other side and was able to win over enough votes to carry the day.

Silver City was elated and the Garden Club, having somehow learned of my intervention on its behalf, insisted that I must drive down and participate in the unveiling and dedication of the sign.

I took advantage of the occasion to visit Mrs. Antrim's grave. While her son, the Kid, is among the most publicized figures in our history, she is scarcely known.

Catherine's early story is quite confused. One tale, which cannot be verified, has her born in Jamaica of Scotch-Irish parents, who later immigrated to New Orleans.

As a young lady, she went to New York and married a William Bonney, who soon afterward died, or was murdered. Her next "husband," Michael McCarty (they probably were not legally wed) soon took to his heels.

Next, according to some sources Catherine was living in Indiana with her two small sons Joseph and Henry McCarty, the latter being the future New Mexico outlaw.

It was in Indiana that a rather shiftless young man named William Antrim became smitten with the widow McCarty. Years later, Governor Miguel Otero in his book on her infamous son would describe Catherine as a handsome woman with "light blue eyes and soft blond hair."

She also had initiative and spunk. In late 1869, she took the children and moved to the new town of Wichita on the Kansas prairie. Antrim followed her.

Catherine opened the City Laundry downtown, bought real estate, and prospered. But by 1871 she was diagnosed with tuberculosis. As she declined over the next two years, a doctor suggested going to the arid Southwest for her health. Soon afterward, the family, including William Antrim, showed up in Santa Fe.[1]

Here on March 1, 1873, Catherine McCarty was married to William Antrim. The Rev. David McFarland performed the service in Santa Fe's adobe First Presbyterian Church northwest of the plaza. The McCarty sons, Joseph and Henry, stood as witnesses.

Before long, the four took the trail for Silver City. That place seemed to have a better climate for the ailing Catherine, and William wanted to do some prospecting.

There the boys attended school and undersized Henry was remembered as having been a good and obedient student. One unconfirmed story claims that Antrim abused his wife, and when Henry caught him at it one day, he knocked him out with a chair.

Catherine Antrim's tuberculosis claimed her life on September 16, 1874. She was only 45 years old, and her adoring son Henry was 14. The boy later said that his step-father's cruelty and his mother's early death were what pushed him into a life of crime. The mistreatment claim is now disputed.

In those days, some folks in Silver City were in the habit of referring to Henry McCarty as "Kid Antrim." When he left the area to ride the desperado trail, he took the alias, William Bonney, the name of his mother's first husband. Because of his slight stature and boyish features, his companions called him Billy the Kid, or just the Kid.[2]

When I stood beside Catherine Antrim's grave a quarter century ago, I recall thinking that had she stayed in Wichita, her son's personal history might have turned out differently. But the move to New Mexico's wild frontier almost guaranteed that Billy the Kid would wind up on the wrong side of the law.

Mrs. Antrim's first gravestone was a simple slab. Fifty years later it was replaced by this granite monument with her first name misspelled.

3

A FIRST JAIL BREAK

In the beginning week of September 1875, a year after the death of his mother, Henry (McCarty) Antrim was arrested by the Grant County Sheriff Harvey Whitehill on the charge of burglary. It seems he had stolen clothes, blankets, and a couple of pistols from a Chinese laundry in Silver City.

Jailed while awaiting action of a grand jury, Henry managed to escape by wriggling up a chimney. The blackened hole was narrow, "yet the lad squeezed his frail slender body through it and gained his liberty," reported Sheriff Whitehill in wonderment.[1]

It is usually said that upon Billy Antrim's flight from jail, he headed straight for Arizona. However, the late Rita Hill once told me that old-timers contended that the young fugitive stopped over for a time in Ralston City (later renamed Shakespeare) near today's Lordsburg, New Mexico. During his short stay,

Stratford Hotel today, Shakespeare, New Mexico. Did Billy Antrim really wash dishes here as legend claims?

he washed dishes in the Stratford Hotel and probably waited tables.

Another story has the Kid taking a side trip north from Silver City to herd sheep on the large ranch of Amado Chaves close to the village of San Mateo.

In 1970 rancher Floyd Lee, who had acquired the Chaves property in the early 20th century, showed me the ruins of "Fort" San Miguel, a fortified sheep camp used by the Chaves family. Billy is

"Fort" San Miguel on the Chaves sheep ranch. (C.F. Lummis photo)

alleged to have stayed there during his brief employment. After earning enough to buy a pony, he went on to Arizona.[2]

Whether either of these incidents—the dish washing and the sheepherding—actually occurred is impossible to say. But they do indicate how eager were people in the past to be able to point to some spot and proclaim, "Billy the Kid slept here."

4

THE LOST YEARS OF BILLY THE KID

Dallas businessman Ramon F. Adams loved the history of the Old West. While reading widely in the subject, his special interests were the cattle trade, cowboy life, and outlaws. Before his death in 1976, he wrote and published twenty-four books on those topics.

I attended Woodrow Wilson High School which was located just a few blocks from Adams' modest residence. But I had not heard of him or his books in those days and, no occasion to seek him out.

Years later, on a visit to Dallas, sometime in the late 1960s, I made a point of paying him a visit. By then I knew his name very well and carried an arm load of books I wanted him to autograph.

Ramon F. Adams at that time was silver-haired, tall, and slightly stooped and, as I recall, we had a pleasant conversation about our mutual fascination with the frontier. Somehow in passing, I mentioned Billy the Kid and he remarked that the young outlaw was one of his favorite historical figures.

Indeed, one of Adams' most popular works is the book, *A Fitting Death for Billy the Kid* (1960). It demolishes many of the old myths that over the years had accumulated around the Kid's life history.

Following my brief meeting with Adams, I chanced upon an obscure article he published in 1929. It dealt with the Kid's "lost years" in Arizona, then one of the least known periods in his bloodstained career.

A street scene in Silver City, New Mexico not long after Billy the Kid's flight. (Museum of New Mexico photo negative #11933)

Born in New York City, the Kid's original name was Henry McCarty. He accompanied his widowed mother west and was present when she married William H. Antrim at Santa Fe on March 1, 1873.

The new couple soon moved to Silver City. Billy would not see Santa Fe again until 1880, when he came back as a prisoner to be jailed on a charge of murder.

Mrs. Antrim died at Silver City in 1874 and without her restraining hand, the boy, now going by the name Billy Antrim, quickly went to the bad.

He became involved in the burglary of a Chinese laundry and was jailed by Grant County Sheriff Harvey Whitehill. However, Billy did not stay caught. He escaped by climbing up a chimney and fleeing across the territorial line into eastern Arizona.

While bits and pieces had long been known about the two years Billy spent there, still there were many gaps in the data. Then in the late 1920s, Ramon Adams chanced to meet an old-timer who claimed he had been a friend of the Kid's in that period and was willing to share his recollections.

The man's name was B. E. Denton, known to his friends as Cyclone. According to Adams, "he was a typical old-time Texas cowboy, uneducated and bighearted. I came to know him well."

Popular 19th century image of Billy the Kid.

Cyclone Denton related that as a youngster off the Texas range he had drifted into eastern Arizona and gone to work for the Gila Ranch. Billy Antrim was one of the cowboys, about 16 years old then.

The two became fast friends, both being of tender age. Of Billy, Denton said: "He was a good cowboy who never shirked his duty. He was always the first one up in the bunkhouse a-hoopin' and a-hollerin,' he was so full of life. It seemed unusual to me because most kid's his age was sleepy-headed."

Billy wasn't afraid of the devil, partly owing to his accuracy with pistols, shooting one in each hand. Cyclone Denton insists that the Kid taught him how to handle a pair of Colts, a skill that years later got him into Buffalo Bill's Wild West Show.

"As I remember Billy, he had light brown hair which he wore long. He was average height and had steady gray eyes that could bore right through you. He was usually smiling, even when he wasn't pleased. Such a smile means danger." Beyond this brief physical description of the Kid, Adams recorded several small anecdotes given him by Denton, and not much else.

The only thing really useful in the account was that it painted Billy as a competent and hard-working young cowboy before he went on to become a celebrated desperado in New Mexico's Lincoln County.

But was Denton's story true? I seriously doubt it. There are numerous inconsistencies in his tale, one being that Billy was already a seasoned gunhandler at this early date. Other evidence suggests that wasn't the case.

In any event, Ramon Adams accepted Cyclone Denton's claim of a close friendship with Billy the Kid. But he wouldn't be the first western writer to have the wool pulled over his eyes by a smooth-talking old-timer who was not above having a little fun.

5

DOBIE AND THE KID

Before his death in 1964, J. Frank Dobie of Austin wrote more than a dozen outstanding books on regional history and folklore. Some of his colleagues went so far as to knight him with the title, "Mr. Southwest."

More a homespun teller of tales than a formal historian or great stylist, Dobie, nevertheless, wrote about simple things in an intelligent and lucid manner.

A lover of western creatures, his writings dealt with longhorns, mustangs, roadrunners, rattlesnakes, coyotes, and horned toads. For him, they were enduring symbols of the region.

Dobie's focus was mainly on Texas. But in his search for lore he occasionally strayed into New Mexico. In 1929, for example, he published a bit on the life and stirring legend of Billy the Kid.

J. Frank Dobie, famed Texas folklorist who wrote about Billy the Kid.

As of that year, people were still actually remembered the Kid. Dobie talked to a few of them, and collected stories from others who themselves had known participants in the Lincoln County War.

From such informal gathering of the facts, Frank Dobie came away with a poor opinion of the famous outlaw. The glamorous myth that had grown up since Billy's death, he decided, did not hold water. That was true even though some of his contemporaries had favorable things to say about him.

Charlie Siringo, for one, told Dobie that back in late April, 1881, he was in command of a party of cowboys near Roswell. Suddenly, a rider appeared with news that the Kid had just escaped jail in Lincoln, after killing two guards.

"One of my men in glee," related Siringo, "yelled, 'Hurrah for Billy the Kid!' and dived into the Pecos River with his boots on."

Even Sheriff Pat Garrett, who gunned down the noted desperado the following July 14 had kind words to say about him. He described Billy as having "pleasant manners and an open-handed generosity." And, he expressed the belief that the dead youth's memory ought not to be clouded by the misdeeds of others then being attributed to him.

Having fairly noted the case for the defense, Frank Dobie takes after the Kid's gilded image with a sledge hammer. In his view, the boy was simply "a killer of men and the product of the Bowery slum." Mention of the Bowery refers to the popular belief that Billy originally came from the back streets of New York City.

"Billy the Kid was more than a common killer and thief, more than a common leach on society," explains Dobie. "He was an uncommon killer, and he was an uncommon thief."

Dobie further notes that the Kid habitually gambled with Blacks and Mexicans, and cheated them. He helped ambush and murder three Apaches, for the sole purpose of stealing their furs and blankets.

"His companions were for the most part ignorant, sordid, vicious toughs," Dobie claims, And he adds, "As for the Kid's polished Don Juan image given him by journalists, its only basis seems to rest on the fact that he danced with a few Mexican girls of the poorer class."

He also relates a story that was suppose to have occurred at the Chisum Ranch on the Pecos. Billy and the camp cook got into a heated argument one evening.

A frying pan with hot grease was sizzling on the fire. The cook grabbed it and threw it at Billy, burning him severely.

The Kid whipped out his pistol and shot the cook dead. Then, as the other cowboys watched in stunned silence, he calmly mounted his horse and rode away.

"Billy the Kid was indisputably brave," Frank Dobie admits. "In fact, in preserving his own life he was a sheer genius. He was probably the quickest man on the trigger after Wild Bill Hickok."

That judgment by Dobie, regarding the Kid's shooting skills, wouldn't hold up today. We know a good deal more about Billy than was known in the 1920s, and it is clear that he was in no way a spectacular marksman or possessed of a lightning draw.

Dobie seemed to think that Billy the Kid became a major folk figure because of one vivid quality: he had "the art of daring." Since he was a youth always on the run and balanced on the edge of a frightful precipice, his life story never loses its appeal for readers.

"For all his faults," concludes J. Frank Dobie generously, "Billy the Kid's nerve never broke."

Tunstall Store (right) in Lincoln, New Mexico. The building originally had a flat roof. (After Otero)

6

A TUNSTALL DOCUMENT

In early November of 1876, a 23-year-old Englishman, John Henry Tunstall, arrived in Lincoln County, New Mexico Territory. He was seeking investments in land and livestock.

Shortly before this, Tunstall had landed in Santa Fe and begun making inquiries about the local economy. He was surprised to see men walking the streets with a pistol strapped to one hip and a knife to the other.

To save money the Englishman put up at the second rate Herlow's Hotel on San Francisco Street. There by chance he met a young attorney, Alexander A. McSween, from Lincoln, who convinced him to try his luck in southeastern New Mexico. It was a decision fated to have profound consequences.

Tunstall soon purchased a ranch on the Rio Feliz and laid plans to open a store in the town of Lincoln. That brought him into competition with the established firm of L. G. Murphy & Co. which was tied to the notorious Santa Fe Ring.

After months of involvement in complex events that formed part of the Lincoln County War, Tunstall was ambushed and killed in February, 1878. That occurred as he rode with some of his cowboys towards Lincoln. One of those hands, Billy the Kid, later sang at the funeral in what was described by the organist as "a sweet tenor voice."

Just a few weeks after first arriving in Lincoln, Tunstall had addressed a letter, with an attached order for goods, to the firm of Otero, Sellar & Co., commission agents, at El Moro, Colorado. That community, located six miles north of Trinidad, was then the southern terminal for the Denver and Rio Grande Western Railroad, and the point at which wagons were loaded for freight shipment throughout New Mexico.

The original documents—the cover letter and order for goods—were discovered by researcher Mark Gardner who brought them to my attention. They are revealing in that they show Tunstall in the process of establishing himself in business at Lincoln.

In the letter to Otero, Sellar & Co., he notes that he has opened an account with the First National

Bank in Santa Fe (with money supplied by his father, a prominent London merchant). And he declares that he will be paying for future goods and freighting costs through that account.

He also holds out a carrot to the company: "If I find your prices to compare sufficiently favorably with those of St. Louis, I will endeavor to do the bulk of my business with you, instead of with that city, as I should thereby save considerable time."

The goods Tunstall ordered were delivered by wagon on May 9, 1877. He used them to furnish and stock his store for its opening in August of that year.

The list of goods, from the order form, provides an interesting view of what a beginning storekeeper needed on the Southwestern frontier.

Tobacco was always in demand, so Tunstall stocked 300 pounds of plug tobacco, meant for chewing. In addition, he had 100 pounds of smoking tobacco, of a brand called "Fruits & Flowers."

A puzzle is why he ordered 1/2 dozen corn brooms. It would seem that transporting such a common item hundreds of miles would hardly be worth the cost.

His order included a number of tools, hardware, and Navy blue flannel cloth for shirts. There was also ample provision for security, suggesting that young Tunstall was already finding Lincoln a lawless place.

For example, he had the company ship him: 1 small jail padlock for the stable and 1 large jail padlock for the corral gate. These were behind Tunstall's store where he kept his own horses when in town and penned the draft stock of freighters making deliveries. His attention to the locks suggests that horse stealing was a serious problem.

As part of his order, Tunstall asked Otero & Seller to send him a suit of clothes, "dark grey in color, heavy tweed" and a sack coat with hip pockets, including a vest to match, and a pair of top boots at $10. These garments likely were for his personal use and not for store stock.

Of special significance, given the violence that followed, was Tunstall's request for "3 Samuel Colts .45 Calibre, blued steel, latest pattern six-shooter." With them he got 500 rounds of ammunition.

We have to wonder whether one of these three Colts was the weapon carried by Tunstall on the day of his murder. His assailant, after wounding him, finished off the young man with a shot from his own pistol.

These Tunstall documents, that I have quoted

from, offer useful background on one of the key figures in the Lincoln County War. Incidentally, the Tunstall Store still stands and is one of the leading attractions in today's historic Lincoln.

7

BLAZING GUNS IN LINCOLN

The late Jack Schaefer, distinguished New Mexico author, used to say that the image of Old West gunmen, facing each other down in the street at high noon and shooting it out after a fast draw, was largely a myth.

Instead of the fair fight, based on a western code of honor, he claimed that back-shooting, skulking, and ambushing more accurately describe the behavior of most of those early- day gun-toters.

Schaefer was probably right. But ironically, his own best-known novel, *Shane*, contained at the end the classic stand-up gunfight in a saloon. That book, and the film made from it, helped keep the false image alive.

On April 1, 1878 there occurred, on the single street in Lincoln, New Mexico a violent episode which bore all the earmarks of knavery and none of nobility.

It formed one of the chapters in the infamous Lincoln County War.

At the root of the trouble were two competing factions, struggling for economic control of that corner of the territory. On one hand was the entrenched power structure, men associated with the L. G. Murphy Store, usually referred to as "The House." County Sheriff William Brady was in the pocket of this bunch.

Sheriff William Brady, gunned down on the streets of Lincoln.

Their foes were led by a wealthy young English developer, John H. Tunstall, and his attorney, Alexander McSween. Tunstall attempted to break The House's business monopoly by setting up a competing store and bank. He also acquired a ranch fifty miles east of Lincoln.

The previous February Sheriff Brady had sent a rump posse out to that ranch to arrest Tunstall on a trumped up charge. The posse returned saying that it had been bringing Tunstall in when he was killed "attempting to escape."

Ranch employees and friends of the Englishman then formed a vigilante group, called the Regulators, to avenge his death. They began tracking down and killing members of the posse.

A member of the Regulators was one of Tunstall's cowboys, Billy the Kid. He had been completely devoted to his boss and showed no mercy in settling scores.

At mid morning on April 1, Sheriff Brady with two of his deputies, George Hindemann and Billy Mathews, along with a couple of others, were walking down Lincoln's central street when they were ambushed.

The shots came from behind a plank gate and

an adobe wall and were fired by the Kid and five of the Regulators. A half dozen or more bullets struck Brady and with a groan he dropped dead where he stood. Hindemann was also mortally wounded. The rest dived for cover.

Seeing the sheriff fall, Billy ran over to the body to retrieve his rifle. It was an engraved English rifle with silver mounting that Tunstall had originally given Billy. Brady had taken it from the Kid on an earlier occasion when he had arrested him.

As the young man bent down for the gun, Deputy Mathews hiding across the street shot him in the seat of the pants. Dripping blood from his rear, Billy dashed back to his friends.

The Regulators now raced for their horses and fled town under a hail of lead. In his delicate condition, Billy the Kid could not sit in a saddle. So, he stayed behind and slipped around to the doctor's office.

Dr. Taylor Ealy cleaned the wound by running a silk handkerchief through the bullet hole. The pain must have caused the young outlaw to bite his lip.

Afterward, a friend of the Regulators hid Billy under the floor boards of the Tunstall store. That's one story. Another, according to historian Joel Jacobson is that the Kid found a hiding place inside a barrel of flour, while a housewife rolled tortillas on the lid.

Billy eventually escaped town and engaged in a series of deadly adventures. By 1881, he was captured and brought to trial in Mesilla for the murder of Sheriff William Brady.

In court he swore that he had not even fired at Brady during the ambush, but rather at Deputy Mathews against whom he had a special grudge. Scholars believe he was probably telling the truth.

The jury paid no attention. It found Billy the Kid guilty and sentenced him to hang. While awaiting the gallows in Lincoln, the outlaw made his daring escape from the courthouse, an event that added gloss to the legend surrounding his name.

It is said that Brady had been warned of an ambush by Billy the Kid, but he paid no attention, saying the Kid would not stoop to that. How wrong he was!

8

A SUSAN WALLACE LETTER

In August of 1878, General Lew Wallace of Indiana was appointed territorial governor of New Mexico. Soon afterward he traveled to Trinidad, Colorado by rail and there, at track's end, changed to a buckboard for the final leg of his trip to Santa Fe.

Upon arrival, he took up residence in the historic old Governor's Palace on the plaza. Wallace discovered to his dismay that the walls were plastered with adobe and the roof leaked. But he made the best of things and a year later he brought out his devoted wife Susan.

Wallace's fame today rests on two things. First, he was the governor who used a strong hand to settle New Mexico's notorious Lincoln County War. And second, he authored the classic novel, *Ben Hur*, set in biblical times and one of America's early best sellers.

A year after taking up his duties, Governor Wallace, accompanied by Susan, set out in his words, "to investigate difficulties in remote regions of the territory." As he told a newspaper reporter, "I suppose few people in the East know that there is an Apache war, led by Chief Victorio, now in progress in New Mexico."

More than 100 settlers had already been killed, "in the most horrible manner," to use Wallace's own words. Among other victims a short time later would be Judge H.C. McComas and family, personal friends of the governor, who were slain on the road near Silver City.

For safety on their journey, Lew and Susan rode in an army ambulance surrounded by a strong guard armed with Winchester rifles. At a small village on the Rio Grande near Socorro, the people turned out and greeted them with amazement.

"Had we been newly raised from the dead, they could not have shown greater awe," he explained. The reason was that all travelers the previous week had been slain on the roads by Apaches.

"We followed the people inside their church," said the governor. "Before the altar were 16 corpses of men, women, and children, some of them shockingly mutilated. In view of this butchery, it is no wonder that they considered our escape a miracle."

The Wallaces soon left the Rio Grande and veered southeast to Fort Stanton in Lincoln County. There, Susan Wallace wrote a detailed and interesting letter to their son back in Indiana. The opening lines of the letter, owing to her harsh criticism of the territory, have become famous. Declared Susan:

"My Dear, —Gen. William Sherman was right. We should have another war with Old Mexico to make her take back New Mexico. I did not believe anything could make me think well of Santa Fe, but this hideous spot, Fort Stanton, does.

Fort Stanton in Lincoln County, visited by Susan Wallace in May of 1879. (National Archives photo)

The couple was lodged in the quarters of the post trader whose cook, according to Susan, was "a Mexican giant with long, straggling black hair." After frying the bacon, she says, he would stand like a huge statue, staring as they ate.

Efforts by Susan's hosts to please her were to no avail. "They sent miles away for a chicken," wrote she, "and when brought and fried by the giant, I could not eat the skinny thing—all bone and fiber. I remarked to the post commandant that this country was not made for civilized man. He agreed."

Of greater interest perhaps are Mrs. Wallace's remarks about that district's most celebrated figure. "The Lincoln County reign of terror is not over and we hold our lives at the mercy of desperadoes and outlaws."

"Chief among them is Billy the Kid. He boasts that he has killed a man for every year of his life." Susan was evidently the first to mention the Kid's boastful claim, and from her letter it was afterward picked up by popular writers and widely used.

She also noted that Billy at that time was threatening to gun down the local sheriff and judge, as well as Governor Wallace. "After these killings," she says, "the Kid swears he will surrender and be hanged.

Those are his words."

"One of my friends," continued Susan, "warned me to close the shutters at evening, so that the bright light of the lamp might not make such a shining mark of the governor who writes till late on *Ben Hur*. Billy has a gang of admirers and followers and they dash up and shoot out the candles."

"This way of living does not suit me. Sweet home in Indiana was never sweeter to my thought than now in this wilderness."

And Susan Wallace drew her letter to a close: "When the *Ben Hur* manuscript is ready we will go to New York with it. How glad I shall be to think there will be no return to this territory!"

9

ELFEGO AND THE KID IN ALBUQUERQUE

It is generally agreed that Elfego Baca, the Old West gunfighter who later became a detective and lawyer, was one of New Mexico's most colorful characters.

In his later years, he enjoyed telling the story of how he and Billy the Kid once went on a spree in Albuquerque.

The adventure began when Elfego at age 17 first met the Kid during a cattle roundup northeast of Socorro. The two became chums and after the branding was finished, they headed for Albuquerque to celebrate.

At Isleta pueblo, they left their horses and rode the rest of the way in to town on a railroad handcar. New Albuquerque, recently built at trackside, was then a wild and lawless place.

Old Town Albuquerque where Elfego Baca says he and Billy the Kid went on a spree. (Albuquerque Museum photo)

The boys, walking the streets, were startled to see a recently arrived Colorado rogue, Milt Yarberry, gun down a hapless citizen. They next moved a mile over to Old Town, which Elfego Baca described as "wide open with liquor and women of all kinds."

"Billy carried a little pistol called a Bulldog Repeater," he said. "It made more noise when fired than a .45 caliber gun."

The pair went into the large and crowded Martínez Saloon where there was dancing, gambling and every other thing. After a few drinks at the bar, they went outside.

The Kid, feeling devilish, fired his pistol in the air. From nowhere appeared Deputy Sheriff Cornelio Murphy.

"I know one of you two did that shooting," he said sharply. But upon searching both young men, he could find no firearm.

"We went back into the Martínez Saloon," related Elfego. "There Billy fired one more shot at the ceiling and the lights went out."

"The deputy ran in and angrily searched us again. But once more he found no gun," Elfego declared. "Later, I asked Billy where he had hidden his pistol. For an answer, he raised his Derby hat and there it was on top of his head. I just smiled."

Until the day he died in 1945, Elfego Baca took great delight in repeating this little tale, always with added embellishments.

However, his recent biographer Larry D. Ball states that while Elfego may have believed his companion was *the* Billy the Kid, in fact he couldn't possibly have been.

Elfego's reference to seeing the Yarberry killing pins the date down to June 18, 1881, at which time the real Billy the Kid was elsewhere. But in the Albuquerque vicinity, then were two other desperadoes—one nicknamed the Texas Kid and the second the Slim Kid.

Either could have been the Kid that Baca, decades later, remembered as Billy. Whether it was a simple mistake on his part or a deliberate fabrication to glorify his own reputation is open to debate.

The only authentic record of Billy the Kid in Albuquerque refers to his passing through town on the train. That happened after his capture by Sheriff Pat Garrett near Fort Sumner and his removal to Santa Fe where he was jailed for a brief period.

Sister of Charity Blandina Segale in her memoirs tells of seeing him incarcerated, shackled and tethered to the floor of his cell.

Billy wrote several urgent letters to Governor Lew Wallace, requesting that he visit him in jail to discuss the legal status of his case. Although he was residing only a few blocks away in the Palace of the Governors, Wallace ignored the pleas.

Finally the Kid was placed on a train south. He was being sent to Mesilla to stand trial on charges of killing in 1878 William Brady, sheriff of Lincoln.

When the train stopped briefly at the Albuquerque depot, a throng of sightseers crowded the platform. They craned their necks for a glimpse of the Kid through the coach window.

The slight young man was handcuffed under the watchful eye of two deputies. He nodded and smiled pleasantly at the crowd, as if he had not a care in the world.

None of the onlookers would have guessed from Billy the Kid's calm expression that he was fully aware he would soon be sentenced to hang.

10

THE STRANGER WORE TWO GUNS

For many years the Spanish-speaking residents of south central New Mexico told this story among themselves. It dealt with a time when outlaws rode the back trails and no man's life or property was safe.

The tale cannot be found in any history of territorial New Mexico. In fact it would have long since been forgotten had not Santa Fe folklorist Frank Applegate recorded it in his notebook during the 1920s.

One evening in April of 1881, a tired and hungry young man trotted his horse along a rough road in the foothills of the Capitan Mountains. Often he cast glances over his shoulder, checking to see if anyone was following him.

As darkness descended, he caught sight of several pinpoints of light up ahead. That would be, he decided, the village of Escondido, so remote and unvisited that its very name translated as The Hidden Place.

The first house the rider came to was also the largest in the community. Here he drew rein and dismounted.

Approaching the door, he knocked loudly. From within came a voice calling, "*Pase adelante!*" (Enter!)

The stranger stepped inside and found himself in a large neat room, softly lighted by the glow from a corner fireplace and a single candle in the center of a plank dining table. A family of three was in the middle of supper.

The father in his mid forties had a strong jaw and the rough hands of a farmer. Next to him sat his wife and across from both, a daughter age 18 who was a beauty with raven hair and lustrous eyes.

They thought the knock was one of their neighbors and were astounded to see this unfamiliar face, and of an Anglo no less. Plus the pair of pistols he wore belted to his waist looked positively unfriendly.

However, when the young man, really a boy, spoke it was in perfect Spanish and his words were filled with courtesy. He had traveled fast and far, and needed lodging for the night and a meal for himself and his mount. For these he offered to pay.

The man hospitably declined payment and seated the newcomer at the table while he went outside to take care of the horse. In his absence, the daughter whispered to her mother that perhaps this boy was a saint in disguise. He certainly resembled the young archangel, San Miguel, in their church.

As their guest finished a bowl of chile stew, the father returned. He announced that the family was going to a baile, or dance, that night and the young man should stay in the house until their return.

"Oh, but I love bailes. I've been to many," said the diner.

A cloud passed over the face of the host and he replied sternly, "No! No! You must not attend the baile. It would not be safe, and I'll tell you why."

And he explained that for several weeks, Escondido had been held captive by a bandido from the plains of Chihuahua, named Ruíz. He had been chased north of the border by soldiers and was here hiding out.

He was a very dangerous man who liked his whiskey, and one villager who crossed him had already been shot down in cold blood. "We are simple farmers, not *pistoleros*," moaned the father, "so Ruíz does as he pleases. Even though you carry guns, young fellow, he would kill you if you went to the dance."

And he added that Ruíz had commanded all the people of Escondido to attend, and it was clear he meant to take the daughter of this household.

"I have no gun," said the father, "but I will defend my child's honor with my last drop of blood." And he pulled back his jacket to reveal a knife thrust into his belt.

The family departed for the dancehall, and five minutes later their guest blew out the candle and followed them in the dark.

He arrived to find the hall already filled. Peering in, he saw a leering Ruíz advancing upon his host, and his wife and daughter. Then the stranger stepped through the door.

The bandido from Mexico saw him first and instantly recognized him from reward posters. "El Chivato," he gasped.

The crowd was electrified. None had ever seen the young man before, but all knew that name.

"All right, Ruíz," said El Chivato quietly. "Walk out of here, ride away, and never come back. And I mean what I say, for I killed two men in Lincoln yesterday."

Lincoln County Courthouse where Billy the Kid killed two deputies on April 28, 1881. (After Otero)

In a flash, Ruíz departed and Escondido was free. Next morning the whole village turned out to watch the boy with two guns mount his horse and bid them adiós. They never saw him again.

Six weeks later at Fort Sumner on the Pecos River, Pat Garrett shot down El Chivato, known to the world as Billy the Kid.

11

SUSAN MCSWEEN

In the annals of New Mexico's Lincoln County War, outlaw Billy the Kid usually receives the lion's share of attention. But another figure, fascinating in her own right, was Susan Hummer McSween, wife of the leader of one of the warring factions.

Born in Gettysburg, Pennsylvania, Susan fled from home to escape parental authority and made her way to the Midwest. There she fell in love with and married a lawyer named Alexander A. McSween, who seemed to have few prospects.

He was practicing in Eureka, Kans. when some difficulty caused the couple to leave hastily in the middle of the night and head west. Months later they showed up (March 5, 1875) in Lincoln, New Mexico, riding in a wagon pulled by a yoke of black oxen.

Susan McSween at home in White Oaks, New Mexico, 1926 (After Otero)

At this time, young Susan was described as tall, redheaded, and having plain features and pop eyes. She was said to be out-spoken and pushy. Her husband himself was aggressive, lacking in tact. Susan had become his fearless supporter in all things.

Alexander learned that there was no lawyer in Lincoln County, so he decided to stay and hang out his shingle. It proved to be a fatal decision. The county was under the thumb of James Dolan who controlled not only local politics but the county economy as well. Further, he was closely allied to the powerful Santa Fe Ring.

Young Englishman John Henry Tunstall arrived at Lincoln in November, 1876 and soon bought a ranch. Alexander McSween became his attorney and business associate. Together they challenged the local power establishment.

In a letter Tunstall mentioned that Susan had acquired many enemies because of her husband's activities. The English newcomer was himself shortly murdered, an act that touched off the horrors of the Lincoln County War.

That tragic episode culminated in the famous Five Days' Battle, or siege of the McSween sprawling residence in Lincoln during July, 1878. One of the defenders was Billy the Kid, who had been a cowboy for Tunstall and remained loyal to his memory.

On the last day, one wing of the house was set on fire and over several hours it spread to other parts of the building. An old story claims that Susan played the piano, heedless of the smoke, so as to inspire the men.

Later, she slipped out and made her way safely through the besiegers' lines. Reaching the camp of Lieutenant Colonel Nathan Dudley, who had ridden over from Fort Stanton with the 9th Cavalry, Susan begged him to stop the violence. Being sympathetic to the anti-McSween faction, Dudley coldly rejected her plea.

Susan McSween then gallantly returned to her doomed home. At day's end, Alexander sat slumped in a chair, in a state of exhaustion and shock. The Kid, who had taken charge, slapped him and pulled his hair, trying to break through the lawyer's mental fog.

The two women and five children in the house were sent out, and soldiers escorted them away. In the night lit by the burning structure, the McSween partisans emerged with guns blazing. Billy the Kid and several others fought their way through and escaped. Alexander and the rest died in the hail of bullets.

One historian has written that Susan's courage and abilities continued to support her after her husband's demise. She stayed in Lincoln for a time, salvaging the wreck of his estate, undismayed by repeated threats against her life.

Finally, she bought land to the west, on the edge of the Tularosa Basin and developed a successful cattle ranch. In 1884 Susan married George Barber, but divorced him seven years later. Upon selling the ranch in 1917 to Senator Albert B. Fall, she had 8,000 cows and owned half interest in a silver mine. Alexander McSween would have been proud of his wife's prosperity.

Moving to the nearby mining town of White Oaks (north of Carrizozo), Susan spent her later years in comfort, enjoying her status as a historical celebrity. Upon her death in 1931 at age 86, Susan McSween Barber was among the last survivors of the Lincoln County War.

Grave of Susan McSween, White Oaks, New Mexico (Pete Klinefelter photo)

Grave of Susan McSween, White Oaks, New Mexico, with a picture of her leaning against the stone. (Pete Klinefelter photo)

12

SHARING A MEAL WITH BILLY THE KID

Harry F. Cummings of Las Vegas, New Mexico some years ago wrote to me saying: "My grandfather witnessed part of the Lincoln County War as a teenager."

"My brothers and I would listen to him telling of his early days and his encounter with Billy the Kid, whenever we visited him in Tularosa. From there, he moved in the mid 1950s to Alamogordo."

Mr. Cummings went on to say that he had several clippings telling of his grandfather Frank Phillips' long career as a cowboy and of his recollections of the bloody war in Lincoln County. He offered to send me copies in case I was interested in writing up the story. Indeed I was!

Frank's father Norris Phillips, I learned, had come to New Mexico before the Civil War and enlisted in the Union Army, probably in one of the volunteer units.

Cowboy Frank Phillips in his later years. (Photo courtesy of Harry F. Cummings)

At war's end, he was mustered out at Fort Sumner and there married Manuela Barella (or Barela). She was perhaps from Puerto de Luna, below Santa Rosa on the Pecos River, for that's where the couple was living when Frank Phillips was born not long afterward.

When he was 12, the family moved to Lincoln

town and the father, Norris, found employment as a tailor for the soldiers at nearby Fort Stanton. In his teens, Frank was sent to school in Doña Ana above Las Cruces.

Once, he and a chum decided to go on an overnight fishing trip up the Rio Grande to the vicinity of Fort Selden. Who should ride into their camp but Billy the Kid, with two companions.

At that date, the Kid had not yet attained the celebrityhood that would come his way in later years. The boys offered to share their pot of campfire stew with the trio of newcomers, who ended up staying the night.

On the following morning, Billy rode into the fort to pick up a pair of spurs at the Sutler's store. Frank elected to tag along.

The little incident that happened there, Frank Phillips never grew tired of repeating. "My eyes nearly popped out," he related, "when I saw the Kid throw down a $20 bill and tell the clerk to keep the change, after picking out his $2.50 spurs."

A year or so later, Frank was back home where he watched events surrounding the so-called "Five Day Battle" at the Alexander McSween house, which proved to be the climax of the Lincoln County War.

Lawyer and merchant McSween with J.H. Tunstall had challenged the notorious Murphy-Dolan faction, which exercised economic control over that corner of New Mexico. McSween and Tunstall's new store appeared as a threat to the old guard's mercantile empire.

Both sides hired gunmen and open conflict erupted. Although only 18 years old, Billy the Kid emerged as a leader among the McSween partisans.

The Five Day Battle began on July 15, 1878, when McSween's foes surrounded him in his house next to the store. Inside with him were some of his men, including the Kid.

The siege lasted until July 19th. The attackers had set fire to the McSween residence, and it slowly spread through the building during that day. In the evening, Billy the Kid announced that they could no longer remain inside amid the smoke.

He led part of the men out a back door. Several were killed, but Billy and four others escaped. A few minutes later, Alexander McSween emerged, but was slain in a hail of gunfire.

Frank Phillips with other Lincoln boys watched the day's events from a safe distance. Years later, when interviewed by historians and journalists, he would say: "McSween died tragically. He came out with a Bible in hand and attempted to surrender. Of course, they shot him down." So far as I am aware, Phillips is the only source to include reference to McSween carrying a Bible.

In his interviews, he also stated that McSween's wife, Susan, who had been watching the battle from across the street, raced to the side of her fallen husband while bullets still flew.

Frank Phillips spent his life as a cowboy. Among others, he worked for famed rancher John Chisum, who ran cattle from Fort Sumner down the Pecos to the Guadalupe Mountains.

Phillips died on February 9, 1960 at age 94. His obituary in an Alamogordo newspaper declared that he was one of the last old-timers who had actually seen Billy the Kid and been present during the Lincoln County War.

13

THE KILLING OF JUAN PATRÓN

In his book *High Noon in Lincoln*, author Robert M. Utley states that Juan Patrón, a participant in the grotesque Lincoln County War, survived that conflict and went on to become speaker of New Mexico's territorial legislature.

According to Utley, Patrón seemed destined for even greater things, perhaps a delegate's seat in the U.S. Congress. But in 1884 his career was cut short when he was shot and killed in a Puerto de Luna saloon.

Patrón's contact with Billy the Kid was both cursory and curious. On. March 21, 1879 the Kid surrendered to Lincoln County Sheriff George Kimbrell, as part of a secret deal he had made with Governor Lew Wallace to gain a full pardon. Initially, he was confined in the store of Juan Patrón, handcuffed, but not otherwise constrained. During the twenty-seven days he spent in Patrón's "custody," the relaxed Billy had "plenty to eat and drink, the best of cigars, and a game of poker with any one, friend or stranger, who chanced to visit [him]."[1]

Although Juan Patrón made a pretense of being neutral in the war, he was known to tilt in favor of the Tunstall-McSween faction. Since Billy the Kid was one of its staunch adherents, Patrón perhaps extended him what support he could. Of equal significance was the fact that Spanish-speaking Billy had a natural affinity for Hispanics.

As Susan McSween, who knew him well, expressed it: "He was universally liked; the native citizens, in particular, loved him because he was always kind and considerate to them."[2] If Patrón shared any of that sentiment, it might explain why the Kid in captivity at his store enjoyed abundant meals and costly cigars.

Juan Patrón was born in Lincoln town about 1855 to a prominent merchant. In his late teens, the five notorious Horrell brothers blew in from Texas. They were as mean a batch of hell-raisers as ever invaded the territory.

On the night of December 20, 1873, the Horrells

rode into Lincoln, bent on terror. A wedding dance was in progress at the courthouse.

The brothers began shooting randomly through the doors and windows. Four men inside were killed and three wounded. One of the dead was Isidro Patrón, father of Juan.

Inheriting the family store, Juan continued to operate it with some success. He was described at this time as a man large and stout who was fond of wearing a Prince Albert coat.

The store and home of Juan Patrón, Lincoln, New Mexico. (After Otero)

One negative thing about him: when Juan Patrón was drinking he became dangerous and tended to pick fights. Local people learned to stay out of his way on those rare occasions.

Through the bloody days of the war, Patrón for the most part managed to stay on the sidelines. Still his life was in peril and a couple of times he was nearly assassinated.

In 1883 he left Lincoln for good and moved to Puerto de Luna on the Pecos River below Santa Rosa. There he opened a large hotel.

On the evening of April 9, 1884, Juan and a companion visited the local saloon for a sociable drink. There are two conflicting versions of what followed.

His friends claimed that Patrón was in a good mood, but soon announced that he was sleepy and ready to go home to bed. About then, Michael Maney, a cowhand from Texas stepped forward and without provocation shot Juan in cold blood.

Maney also wounded a bystander before retreating through the door. He leaped on his horse and headed out of town.

Strangely, the killer came in and surrendered the next day. Appearing before the local justice of the peace, he was ordered sent to Las Vegas as there was no jail in Puerto de Luna.

The story began to circulate that Patrón's killing had been arranged by some of the kingpins in Lincoln. They thought he knew too much about the recent war and wanted him out of the way.

Once in Las Vegas, Maney gave his own version of the circumstances that led up to the Patrón shooting. He insisted that he had been on friendly terms with the deceased, and the start of the trouble was not his doing.

On the fateful night, the cowboy claimed that Juan had been drinking and he took exception when he noted that Maney was wearing a pistol. Patrón declared that anyone who would wear a pistol was a damned coward.

Then Patrón, who was unarmed, said he would go home, get his gun, and come back to demonstrate his shooting ability. Upon returning, he had a six-shooter stuck in the belt of his pants.

According to Maney, when he saw Juan Patrón reach for his gun, he feared for his life and so he shot him. He stoutly denied having been hired by anyone to do this killing.

At his court hearing, Michael Maney pleaded "not guilty." The first trial ended in a hung jury. Evidently, the jurors were unable to sort out the truth from the conflicting testimony of witnesses.

A second trial was scheduled. But the defendant's lawyer sought and got a change of venue to Santa Fe. The accused never made it to the capital.

Even though he was wearing irons, he managed to escape during a visit to the privy. Someone had cut a hole in the roof providing an exit. Maney's brother, who had been seen in town, was suspected.

New Mexico's territorial governor Lionel A. Sheldon immediately put up a $500 reward for fugitive Maney's recapture. But no one ever claimed it.

Most folks in the Pecos Valley assumed that Patrón's killer had high-tailed it back to Texas. Governor Sheldon thought so too and asked the governor of that state to find and return him. But he never got a response.

Had not Juan Patrón's life briefly touched the Lincoln County War, his career and death would be wholly forgotten to day.

14

THE GOVERNOR AND THE KID

Miguel Antonio Otero served as the first Hispanic governor of the U.S. Territory of New Mexico, from 1897 to 1907. He was appointed to office by President William McKinley.

Long after his retirement from politics, Governor Otero wrote and published his memoirs in three volumes, a major contribution to New Mexico history. But he also published a biography in 1936 titled, *The Real Billy the Kid*.

His aim in that book, he proclaimed, was to write the Kid's story "without embellishment, based entirely on actual fact." Otero had known the outlaw briefly and also the man who killed him in 1881, Sheriff Pat Garrett.

The author recalled Garrett saying that he regretted having to slay Billy. Or as he bluntly put it, "It was simply the case of who got in the first shot. I happened to be the lucky one."

Miguel Otero was age 21, and just a month older than the young desperado, when he first saw the Kid at Las Vegas, New Mexico. That was two days before Christmas in 1880.

Sheriff Garrett's posse had brought in Billy and his gang after capturing them at Stinking Springs. Las Vegas was the nearest railhead where the prisoners, in chains, could be placed on a train for Santa Fe.

As it happened, a mob gathered at the station with violent intent. One of the gang members, Dave Rudabaugh, had earlier murdered a local jailer and the crowd was eager to seize him and perform a lynching.

The Sheriff managed to get the outlaws onto the train but a throng of people on the tracks prevented its departure. He then mounted the platform and made a speech, declaring that, if necessary, he would arm the prisoners so they could defend themselves.

The explosive situation was actually defused by Otero's father, Miguel, Sr., a prominent politician and businessman. Speaking eloquently in Spanish, he persuaded the townsmen to withdraw and let the law take its course.

Miguel A. Otero (right) and his brother Page B. Otero (left), about 1880. (After Otero)

"The Kid was disappointed that the mob did not attack the car since it would unquestionably have resulted in his escape," observes Otero in his biography. And he describes him as "a short, slender young man with large front teeth, giving a chronic grin to his expression."

Having witnessed the stirring events at the train station, Miguel, Jr., and his brother Page got permission from their father to go on board for the ride to the capital. On the way they visited with Billy and Dave Rudabaugh, even becoming a bit chummy.

According to Otero, "In Santa Fe we were allowed to see the Kid in jail, taking him cigarette papers, tobacco, chewing gum, candy, pies and nuts. He was very fond of sweets and asked us to bring him all we could."

By all accounts Billy the Kid was much adored by New Mexico's Hispano population. Otero asserts that he was considerate of the old, the young, and the poor. And he was loyal to his friends.

He quotes a Mrs. Jaramillo of Fort Sumner who testified that "Billy was a good boy, but he was hounded by men who wanted to kill him because they feared him."

Further, Martin Chaves of Santa Fe stated: "Billy was a perfect gentleman with a noble heart. He never killed a native citizen of New Mexico in all his career, and he had plenty of courage."

Otero was especially admiring of Billy because

as a boy in Silver City, "he had loved his mother devotedly." Such praise must be viewed in the context of the times. Other people, of course, saw Billy as an arch-villain.

Otero's biography, *The Real Billy the Kid*, was printed at the height of the Depression in a very small edition. One scholar recently made a computer check and could locate only 118 copies preserved in libraries, world-wide!

An unknown and doubtless limited number remain in private collections. I have a copy in my personal library, obtained long ago at considerable cost. I regard the volume as a prime treasure.

In 1998 Arte Público Press of Houston published a paperback edition of Otero's work, its first reprinting. A note in the new, politicized introduction claimed that Governor Otero's narrative had "challenged the image of Billy the Kid as rendered by the Euroamerican colonial power structure," and thus his text had not been as popular as Pat Garrett's book or those by other Anglo-American writers. Therefore, it had taken all these years for Otero's voice on Billy the Kid to be reintroduced to the public!

Pat Garrett stalking Billy the Kid

Sheriff Garrett as he appeared in 1882. (Contemporary engraving)

15

PAT GARRETT'S BOOK

When Lincoln County Sheriff Pat Garrett ended Billy the Kid's life on the night of July 14, 1881 with a shot in the dark, he was catapulted at once into stardom in the annals of Western history.

The killing occurred at old Fort Sumner on the Pecos River. Garrett by pure chance had encountered the Kid in a darkened room of the Pete Maxwell house. As the unsuspecting Billy entered, he was cut down without warning.

Before that fateful night, there was not much in Garrett's career to suggest he was headed for a place in the history books. Alabama-born in 1850, he worked as a cowboy and buffalo hunter in Texas. By 1878 he had drifted to the Pecos in eastern New Mexico.

Perhaps craving excitement, Pat Garrett ran for sheriff of wild Lincoln County in the fall of 1880. He was elected. Winning the office put him on a collision course with the outlaw Billy.

After the sensational shooting at Fort Sumner, there were many in the New Mexico territory who proclaimed Sheriff Garrett a hero. But the Kid had his share of friends and many of them stepped forward to level some harsh criticism against the lawman.

Among them was Deluvina Maxwell, a Navajo servant in the Maxwell household. She had been especially fond of the slain desperado.

New Mexico historian William A. Keleher, whom I interviewed in 1966, claimed that Deluvina had gone into the room carrying a candle soon after the gunfire stopped. She wanted to help Billy, but it was too late.

Supposedly, she snarled at Pat Garrett, "You SOB! You didn't have the nerve to kill him to his face." Her implication was that Garrett had staged a cowardly ambush, which was not the case at all.

Garrett's biographer, Leon Metz of El Paso, states that their confrontation took place not on the night of the shooting but rather the next day during Billy's funeral. Deluvina was tearful when she dressed down the sheriff.

It soon became clear that while Pat Garrett was an instant celebrity, he had also come away, at least in some quarters, with a negative image.

To address that problem, he began thinking about a book to give the public his side of the story. With the rising popular interest in Billy the Kid, he also thought a little money could be made from such a publication.

Prominent New Mexicans who lauded the removal of the troublesome Kid took up a collection of $1,500 and presented it to Garrett. But he quickly wasted the sum on whiskey and gambling. He was prepared, therefore, to try for some book profits.

The editor of the Santa Fe *New Mexican*, Charles Greene, offered to publish a Garrett volume if the sheriff could find someone to ghost write it for him.

Pat enlisted his good friend Marshall Ashmun (Ash) Upson, a journalist, to do the job. Upson cranked out a manuscript and it was published in 1882 under the title *The Authentic Life of Billy the Kid*.

The little book, issued in blue paper covers with ads on the last few pages, was scarcely a bestseller. Indeed, Metz declares that it was a financial flop.

About 1902 Southwestern author Earle Forrest walked past the *New Mexican* office in the capital and observed a bushel basket full of copies of Garrett's book sitting on the sidewalk.

THE AUTHENTIC LIFE
— OF —
BILLY THE KID,

THE NOTED DESPERADO
OF THE SOUTHWEST,

WHOSE DEEDS OF DARING AND BLOOD HAVE
MADE HIS NAME A TERROR IN

NEW MEXICO,
ARIZONA & NORTHERN MEXICO.

— BY —

PAT F. GARRETT,
SHERIFF OF LINCOLN COUNTY, N. MEX.

BY WHOM
HE WAS FINALLY HUNTED DOWN &
CAPTURED BY KILLING HIM.

☞ A FAITHFUL, INTERESTING NARRATIVE ☜

SANTA FE, NEW MEXICO:
NEW MEXICO PRINTING & PUBLISHING CO.,
1882

Title page of the first edition of Pat Garrett's book.

A sign above the basket offered the copies at 25 cents apiece. He plucked out one, took it inside and paid his quarter. Later, after reading the stirring account, he returned to buy several more.

But the basket was no longer in sight. Inquiring, he found someone had purchased the lot and carried all the books away in a wheelbarrow. He never learned where they had gone.

Curious, I checked with a noted Santa Fe bookseller. I wanted to know what Garrett's *The Authentic Life of Billy the Kid*, a first edition, would bring on today's book market.

Quoting from a standard guide to pricing, the dealer informed me that the blue-backed volume was worth now $4,000 or more. Exact value, he told me, is difficult to determine since no copy has come up for sale in recent years.

Wouldn't Garrett have been astonished if he could have seen into the future and known what his 25-cent book would fetch one day?

The young British adventurer R. B. Townshend as he appeared during his early days in New Mexico.

16

AN ENGLISHMAN MEETS BILLY

Richard B. Townshend was a bright, sensitive young Englishman who won a scholarship to Trinity College, Cambridge, and graduated from there in 1865.

Being a romantic sort with an inborn love of adventure, he decided to immigrate to America and attempt to make his fortune in the Wild West.

A year later, he landed in the Colorado Territory and went to ranching. Late in life, back in England, he published three books on his frontier experiences.

One of the most interesting of these involved a business venture that took him through New Mexico in 1879. Not far from his ranch, the mines in Leadville, Colorado had boomed and work mules were in great demand. So Townshend hired several herders and taking a chuck wagon he headed south to buy Mexican mules in the brush country of Texas east of the Pecos River.

Coming back with a large herd, he began climbing the Pecos Valley in eastern New Mexico. Above today's Carlsbad, he encountered a cattleman named Mr. Beckford,[1] known as a rough customer. According to rumor, he had shot his own son-in-law for not obeying him.

The two camped together several days and became quite friendly. Townshend wrote: "Evenings Beckford was careful never to step into the light of the campfire, fearing a shot from the darkness."

"He bragged to me that he was a civilized man because he had brought in a piano by wagon as a gift for his daughter. I didn't have the nerve to tell him that a piano hardly made up for shooting his daughter's husband."

This was just the time that saw the winding down of the Lincoln County War. As the two men parted, Richard Townshend received a warning to watch for highwaymen and rustlers along the Pecos.

"The worst of them is a youngster known as Billy the Kid," he was advised. Mr. Beckford claimed to be his friend and gave Townshend a letter to Billy in case they should meet.

A week later, below Fort Sumner, they did. The Englishman was alone in camp with his cook while the hired men were out with the herd.

Without warning four heavily armed men surrounded them. They were the most evil looking crew that Richard had ever seen. His first inclination was to go for his rifle, but quickly realized that if he did the intruders "would have me for toast." Thus, he decided on diplomacy.

"Good day, gentlemen," said I, trying to look pleasant. "Won't you get off your horses and have some dinner?"

The quartet accepted gruffly, swung down from their saddles and came to the fire. They were dressed in typical cowboy style and wore heavy leather chaps. Three of the men each carried a Winchester and pistol and had two full cartridge belts buckled around their waists.

The fourth man was armed with two rifles, a 16-shot Winchester and a Sharps .45 calibre, popularly called a buffalo gun because of its usefulness in long range shooting. This fellow, who spoke with a thick accent and seemed to be the leader, Townshend described as "a giant in form, with a strong, hard cruel face and the shifty eyes of a wolf."

"Is it safe for us to eat in this camp?" he growled. At first Townshend was not sure what he meant.

The new arrivals sat by the fire, placing the rifles on their laps, ready for instant use. They also arranged themselves facing one another, so as to watch each other's backs. Without a doubt, these were dangerous customers.

The cook served bacon, biscuits and coffee, giving his boss his meal last. The outlaws made no move to eat until they saw Townshend begin. Then in an instant he understood the meaning of that earlier question: "Was the food safe?" These mule thieves were afraid of being poisoned!

As soon as he had finished, the evil-faced giant stood up and announced, "Let's go on to the herd."

The smallest of the four told Richard that he had better go with them. "He was boyish looking, not more than 20," according to Townshend, "and had a restless eye like that of an untamed animal in a cage. His tone was less truculent than the giant's."

As they rode out on the plain, it became clear that the man from Colorado was a prisoner. The boyish one rode beside him and asked all kinds of questions about the mules.

Upon approaching the herd, the party came to a

stop. "It had begun to dawn on me," Townshend wrote afterward, "that this insignificant boyish person was the real leader, and not the big fellow after all."

His conclusion was confirmed when the youngster abruptly asked, "What'll you take for the lot?" The answer was, "Those mules are not for sale."

The giant now chimed in and declared that their intention was to shoot up the outfit and take what they wanted. And he added, " 'Bout time for you to quit yer foolin' around, Kid."

Suddenly, Mr. Townshend got the picture. "Kid! Kid! Of course! Thick-headed idiot I had been not to see. This was the man himself, . . . the young ruffian Beckford had told me of."

Fishing in his pocket, Richard found the crumpled letter. Passing it over to the Kid, he explained: "My friend Mr. Beckford told me I was liable to meet you along the Pecos and this message of his might be of use."

The Kid read the words slowly and then smiled, hiding any disappointment he may have felt. "Mr. Beckford is a friend of mine, too. I hope you get these mules safe to Leadville and a good price, too. If anybody along the road wants to interfere with you, just refer 'em to Billy the Kid."

Richard Townshend summed up his narrow escape with these words: "I never was so glad to see anything in my life as the backs of those four outlaws riding off."

Young Townshend profitably sold his mules in Leadville and went on to other adventures. After many years in the Southwest, he returned to England and married.

His final home was at Oxford. Under its spires he wrote up his reminiscences and also translated from Latin the works of the Roman historian Tacitus. Richard Baxter Townshend died in 1923 at age 77, outlasting Billy the Kid by 42 years.

17

SOME BILLY THE KID IMPOSTERS

A story has long circulated in southern Santa Fe County that local resident Richard B. Williams on his death bed in 1934 confessed to friends that in reality he was Billy the Kid.

The standard account of the Kid's demise is, of course, well-known. It is generally acknowledged that Sheriff Pat Garrett shot him to death at old Fort Sumner on the night of July 14, 1881. But almost from the beginning, doubts surfaced in some quarters that it was so.

One explanation given is that the sheriff in the dark accidentally killed the wrong man, a young vagrant named Billy Barlow. A cover-up followed, Barlow being hastily buried under a wooden cross reading "Billy the Kid."

There seemed to be little about Richard B. Williams that connected him to the famous outlaw.

True, he was short of stature and had blue eyes like Billy, and always carried a gun. But that was scarcely enough to verify that he was Billy the Kid.

If the real Billy did in fact survive his alleged slaying in 1881, the question then becomes this: Were any of the several elderly men, Williams among them, who later claimed to be the infamous desperado able to produce evidence confirming their identity? The simple answer is no.

The odd phenomenon of certain old-timers wishing to hijack the name of a prominent outlaw is not confined to Billy the Kid yearners. At least six different men over the years tried to steal Jesse James's name and reputation after his violent death. The best explanation perhaps is that such phonies act to bring a little excitement and notoriety into their otherwise humdrum lives.

Today, the two pre-eminent pseudo-Billys remain John Miller and Ollie L. "Brushy Bill" Roberts. Books have been written about both men, which lay out the "evidence" for their individual pretensions.[1]

John Miller, a.k.a. Billy the Kid, after his supposed flight from Fort Sumner, headed for Las Vegas where he soon married a New Mexican woman. After some shifting around, the Millers settled on a homestead tract in the Zuni mountains of western New Mexico and went to ranching.

John's life thereafter was anything but spectacular. It was filled mainly with work, raising cattle. In time, all of his neighbors seemed to know that "he was Billy the Kid."

John Miller and his wife adopted a Navajo boy and raised him. This youngster took the name Max Miller. The Navajo people, in their own language, called him "Son of Billy the Kid."

Author and former sheep rancher Abe Peña now lives in Grants. He met Max in the 1960s and once straight-out asked him if his father was Billy the Kid. Max gave a vague answer without admitting anything. But according to Abe Peña, he told others that he *was* the son of Billy the Kid.[2]

Toward the end of his life, John Miller moved to Buckeye, Arizona and worked at farming. He died in Prescott on November 7, 1937.

The most serious claimant to being Billy the Kid was Texas resident Brushy Bill Roberts. In 1950 he set out for Santa Fe with his lawyer William V. Morrison to seek a full pardon for all his crimes from New Mexico Governor Thomas J. Mabry.

Brushy Bill Roberts, claiming to be 91 year-old Billy the Kid, meets New Mexico Governor Thomas J. Mabry, November 30, 1950 to ask for a pardon. (Museum of New Mexico photo negative #87297. Photographer: Harold D. Walter)

Mr. Morrison had arranged a private interview with Mabry in the Governor's Mansion, so that Brushy Bill, now 91, could have his say in a non-threatening atmosphere. However, at the meeting were reporters, photographers, armed police officers and historians called in by the governor to judge the evidence. Roberts became frightened and flustered, fearing he might yet be hanged. To simple questions he gave confusing answers. The event proved a fiasco.

Afterward, the governor issued a statement declaring: "I am taking no action on this application for a pardon because I don't believe this man is Billy the Kid."

A few months later, Brushy Bill Roberts back home in Hico, Texas suffered a heart attack on the street, collapsed on the hood of a parked car and died.

To this day, true believers continue to insist that Brushy Bill was, indeed, the Kid. That flies in the face of overwhelming contrary evidence. During his interview, Governor Mabry pointed out one of the most obvious contradictions. He told Roberts that, besides bearing no resemblance to Billy the Kid, he appeared to be in his seventies rather than his nineties, as he claimed. Roberts blithely responded that he was well-preserved for his age because he had always taken care of his health.

Even more telling were the results of a computer project by the Lincoln County Heritage Trust, begun in 1988. Through technical analysis, the only authentic image of the Kid was compared with a photograph of Roberts. It showed that the two images were not of one and the same man.

Brushy Bill's relatives in Texas have been quoted in the press as denying that he was Billy the Kid. They refer to family records placing his birth in East Texas in 1879, far too late for him to qualify as Billy. A niece has stated that when she was growing up, her uncle related to her all sorts of fanciful yarns about his association with the Jesse James gang, the bandit queen Belle Star, Pancho Villa, and his enlistment in Teddy Roosevelt's Rough Riders.

"I knew it was just talk," she said.

19

DID JESSE JAMES MEET BILLY THE KID?

After New Mexico's Billy the Kid, Missouri's Jesse James was probably the most famous outlaw of the Old West. He and his brother Frank were raised by their mother, Zeralda, a southerner who owned slaves.

During the Civil War, the young James boys rode with the guerrilla leader Bloody Bill Anderson, who committed ruthless crimes in the name of the Confederacy. From that experience, they gained a taste for outlawry that lasted beyond the war.

Historian Dan L. Thrapp says that Jesse and Frank took part in 12 bank robberies, 7 train hold ups, 4 stagecoach robberies, and assorted other unlawful acts, including the hold up of the Kansas City Fair in 1872.

Their most disastrous escapade, with a gang of eight, occurred in 1876, in a raid on the bank at

The young Jesse James.

Northfield, Minnesota. The teller and a citizen were killed, but the assailants were all either shot down or captured, except for Frank and Jesse who escaped wounded back to Missouri. The governor of that state put a $10,000 price on their heads.

The story has long circulated that Jesse James paid a brief visit to New Mexico in late July of 1879. Historians have doubted the tale, while admitting that his whereabouts at that time are unknown. So in fact, it very well could be true.

Albuquerque journalist and author Howard Bryan, in his book *Wildest of the Wild West* (1988), gives a quote from the *Las Vegas Optic*, dated December 8, 1879. It reads: "Jesse James was a guest at the Las Vegas Hot Springs from July 26th to 29th. Of course it was not generally known." That brief public notice, not printed until six months after Jesse's supposed visit, is still a strong bit of evidence.

But even beyond that, we have the testimony of two eyewitnesses, prominent citizens of the day, who claimed to have met and talked with Jesse James at the Hot Springs on that occasion.

One of them was Miguel Antonio Otero, son of a wealthy merchant. Miguel later became governor of the New Mexico Territory and published a memoir titled *My Life on the Frontier,* in which he describes his accidental meeting with Jesse.

Otero says that at Hot Springs, located in the mountains six miles north of Las Vegas, was a place called The Old Adobe Hotel, which included a row of bath houses. A couple from Missouri, Scott and Minnie Moore, ran the establishment.

Mrs. Moore served fine Sunday dinners that attracted folks from miles around. Miguel Otero was often one of their guests, and that's how he happened to meet Jesse James.

Scott Moore, as it turned out, had been a boyhood chum of the James brothers back in Missouri. Jesse felt safe in his hotel while he looked over the surrounding country, with an eye to finding a safe haven where he could bring and settle his family.

"In appearance and dress the man I saw was far from suggesting a noted desperado," wrote Otero. "He was of medium height, his eyes were blue and rather severe, and he wore a short Prince Albert coat. His manner was pleasant, though noticeably quiet and reserved. And his demeanor was so gentlemanly that I found myself liking him immensely."

Curiously, another individual, writing in his memoirs, claimed to have met Jesse during Sunday dinner at the Hot Springs. He was Doctor Henry F. Hoyt, a young physician who was wandering the West, and happened to be in Las Vegas at that time.

Dr. Henry F. Hoyt

When he walked into the dining room, he saw Billy the Kid at a table with two men. Dr. Hoyt had known the Kid earlier at Tascosa in the Texas Panhandle and recognized him immediately.

They greeted each other and Billy introduced one of his table mates as a "Mr. Howard" from Tennessee. Jesse James often went by the alias Thomas Howard. Only later did Hoyt learn that he was the notorious Jesse James.

According to him, Jesse made Billy the Kid a tentative proposition, "that they join forces and hit the trail together." But, as Hoyt tells it, Billy was never a train or bank robber. So he turned down the proposal.

At the dining table, Dr. Hoyt caught a quick glimpse of Jesse James's left hand, which the outlaw usually kept gloved. And he noted that the end of the index finger was missing. Afterward, he learned how it had been lost.

When Jesse was 15 years old and riding with Anderson, he had accidentally shot off the finger while cleaning his six-shooter. From a religious family, he had been brought up not to curse. But as his bleeding hand was quite painful, he shook it and muttered through clenched teeth, "Dingus! Dingus!"

The other outlaws at once gave him the nickname of Dingus, and he was called that by close friends and associates to the end of his life.

It is odd that Otero fails to mention Billy the Kid being at the Old Adobe Hotel on this occasion. Kid scholars, in fact, believe the young desperado was hiding out in southern New Mexico and couldn't have been in the Las Vegas area.

Dr. Hoyt, however, states that he had slipped in to see the new train whose rails had reached Las Vegas only two weeks earlier. Thus, the Kid's meeting with Jesse James was by pure chance.

After three days, Jesse left town, returning east by rail. So far as is known he never visited New Mexico again. Three years later he was killed by one of his outlaw pals, Robert Ford, for the reward.

Pete Maxwell house, Fort Sumner, New Mexico. The Kid was slain in the corner room at left, behind the tree. (After Otero)

19

A GRAVE QUESTION: WHERE IS BILLY BURIED?

Since virtually everything in Billy the Kid's personal history is mired in controversy and surrounded by misinformation, it should come as no surprise that his grave—its exact location, contents, and the story of its markers and monuments—should also be the subject of contention.

One thing not in dispute is that only by pure accident did the Kid blunder into Pete Maxwell's darkened bedroom at Fort Sumner on that fateful night of July 14, 1881, at the very moment his nemesis Sheriff Pat Garrett was there. Had Billy's timing been slightly different, his death might have been postponed. Reaching the Maxwell house mere minutes earlier or minutes later, he could well have had a fighting chance, or even missed Sheriff Garrett altogether. But his own destiny prescribed that it was not to be.

Engraver's fanciful image of Garrett slaying the Kid in Pete Maxwell's bedroom.

The set of circumstances that ultimately brought Billy the Kid to his premature grave in the Fort Sumner cemetery began with Pete Maxwell's father, Lucien Bonaparte Maxwell. Through a fortunate marriage, adroit business dealings, and some luck, he acquired possession of an old Mexican land grant whose vast extent made him one of the largest land holders in the nation.

This grant, sprawling across northeastern New Mexico and into Colorado, Lucien sold to a group of American and European investors in the second half of 1870. A month later, he purchased the buildings of abandoned Fort Sumner from the War Department for $5,000. The military reservation surrounding the fort remained in War Department hands until 1871, when the land, except for the cemetery, was transferred to the Interior Department.[1]

Lucien Maxwell brought his family to Fort Sumner and moved into one of the officers quarters, after considerable remodeling of the structure. With him from the old grant had come some forty additional families, mainly native New Mexicans and Indians who took up residence or opened small businesses in other adobe buildings within the fort. Together, they formed a rather loose and free-wheeling community, one in which Billy the Kid and some of his lawless companions made friends and felt at ease.[2] An additional attraction for the Kid were the young women of the place, especially Lucien's youngest daughter, Paulita.

Upon Lucien Maxwell's death in 1875, he was buried in the southeast corner of the military cemetery, located a short distance southeast of the fort. Leadership of the amorphous settlement then passed to son Pete Maxwell, who lacked his father's forceful personality. In fact, before his own passing in 1898,

Pete had developed an alcohol problem and squandered much of the family wealth. He too was buried in the Fort Sumner cemetery, next to his father.[3]

Since his escape (April 28) from incarceration in the Lincoln County Courthouse, Billy the Kid had been hiding out in sheep camps on the plains east of Fort Sumner. When he came into the fort on the evening of July 14 for a social visit, he ran straight into his fatal encounter with Sheriff Garrett, who had just arrived from Lincoln with two deputies.

The sheriff went to ask Pete Maxwell if the Kid was anywhere in the area, while Billy arrived to ask his friend Pete for permission to carve a steak from a heifer slaughtered earlier in the day. In the Maxwell bedroom, Garrett shot first and Billy the Kid dropped dead from a bullet that passed near the heart.

The sound of gunfire brought members of the Maxwell household and neighbors to the scene. One version of what followed has the corpse being carried soon afterward to the Maxwell carpenter shop across the parade ground where it was placed on a bench (or plank). Friends of Billy gathered there and held a candle-lit *velorio*, or traditional wake, throughout the night. A different scenario would have us believe that the body was left where it fell until the next morning, where a coroner's jury summoned by Garrett was able to view it in place.

On the morning after the shooting, women led by the Navajo Indian servant Deluvina Maxwell washed Billy and combed his hair. Since the shirt he had been wearing was blood-stained and had two holes in it, front and back, Pete Maxwell by one account donated an over-sized shirt of his own, which had to be pinned up in the back to make it fit the slim Kid.[4]

An elderly Deluvina Maxwell. (After Otero)

A P. "Paco" Anaya remembered it differently in 1931 when he wrote down his recollections of the funeral. According to him, Garrett had handed "Pedro" Maxwell $25 and told him to visit Manuel Abreu's store and buy all new clothes for Billy: "a beige suit, a shirt, an undershirt, shorts, and a pair of stockings." Maxwell did so. Then Anaya and several others clothed the corpse. Pat Garrett himself would say: "The body was neatly and properly dressed."[5]

After measuring Billy, Jesús Silva hammered together a coffin the morning of the 15th, then he helped Vicente Otero dig the Kid's grave in the military cemetery. Those two, plus Paco Anaya were reportedly three of the pallbearers.[6]

The funeral was held the same afternoon with practically all Fort Sumner residents in attendance. Store-keeper Manuel Abreu's two-horse wagon bore the coffin to the burial ground. In the absence of a clergyman, Antonio Savedra, who had served as a member of the coroner's jury, led the throng in prayers as Henry McCarty, alias William Bonney, alias Kid Antrim, but known to the world as Billy the Kid, was lowered with ropes into his grave."[7]

Philip J. Rasch has written that "if ever a body rested uneasily in its grave, it was the Kid's." He was referring to a series of articles in the *Las Vegas Daily Optic* that appeared soon after the burial. They indicated that grave robbers were already plundering Billy the Kid's remains.[8]

The first *Optic* story, dated July 25, 1881, announced that a friend of the paper, L. W. Hale of Fort Sumner, had sent the editor the genuine index finger of Billy the Kid. It was identified as the trigger finger which "has snapped many a man's life into eternity."

The grisly trophy was pickled in a jar of alcohol and placed on an office desk for public viewing. "If the rush continues," said the editor, "we shall purchase a small tent and open a side show to which complimentary tickets will be issued to our personal friends."

A few weeks later, the *Optic* ran another story entitled, "The Kid Kidnapped." Noting that the outlaw had been placed in the abandoned cemetery at Fort Sumner, it reported that five days after burial a fearless "skelologist" had dug up the body and carried it off in a wagon.

"The stiff was brought to Las Vegas, arriving here at two o'clock in the morning, and was slipped quietly into the private office of a practical sawbones, who by dent of diligent labor and careful watching to prevent detection, boiled and scraped the skin off the pate so as to secure the skull, which was seen by a reporter last evening."

"The body," continued the newspaper, "was covered with dirt in a corral, where it will remain until decomposition shall have robbed the frame of its meat. Then the body will be dug up again and the skeleton fixed up—hung together by wires and varnished with shellac to make it presentable."

"The skeleton of a crack frontiersman does not grow on every bush, and the bones of such men as the Kid are hard to find. The skull is already 'dressed' and is considered quite a relic in itself."

And the article concluded, "The index finger of the right hand, it will be remembered, was earlier presented to the *Optic*. As this member has now been sold to an easterner, the skeleton will not be complete in its fingers. But the loss is so trivial that it will hardly be noticeable."

One last chapter in this gruesome business appeared in the paper on the following September 19, in an article headlined, "A Desperado's Darling."

It seems that young Miss Kate Tenny of Oakland, California had been smitten with Billy merely through stories about him in the press. Reading that the *Optic* had his index finger in pickle, she wrote and asked for it.

Replied the *Optic*: "We have written Miss Tenny a sorrowful letter, full of touching condolence and broke the news gently that we had just sold our relic of her lover for $150 cash. We will see that physician who was fortunate enough to secure Billy's stiff and will present a request for some part of the Kid's skeleton—a shank bone, or something of that kind, which we will send to the broken hearted maiden as a lasting memento of her dead lover's former greatness." [9]

The macabre affair of poor Billy's remains, spread across the pages of one of the territory's leading newspapers, strikes us today, not only as highly distasteful, but as bordering on the barbaric. Less than a year after publication of these news features on the dispersal of the Kid's body parts, Pat Garrett in his book made vehement denials that any of it was true. Only "credulous idiots" could fall for such nonsense, he asserted.

The sheriff went on to say that "The banks of the Pecos are dotted from Fort Sumner to the Rio Grande with unmarked graves, and the skeletons are of all sizes, ages, and complexions. Any showman of ghastly curiosities can resurrect one or all of them, and place them on exhibition . . . as the Kid, with no one to say him nay."[10]

The *Daily Optic* partially redeemed itself on January 16, 1882 when it ran a more sober and factual story on the condition of the Fort Sumner cemetery. The author, a correspondent of the paper, was able to provide readers with details based on his firsthand observations.

The one acre cemetery then was surrounded by what was once a good adobe wall, but through neglect and decay it had disintegrated, leaving only an outline on the ground. At the main entry on the north, visitors stepped over the ruins of a handsome gate that had collapsed.

Inside, to the left in the northeast corner, rested the unmarked graves of four rustlers, including the Kid's two "pals," Charlie Bowdre and Tom O'Folliard (misspelled O'Fallion in the article). To the right of the entrance, one found the grave of Billy the Kid, marked by a plain board, with the stenciled letters: "Billy the Kid." According to surviving tradition, his gravesite was 25 feet to the right as one entered the gate.[11]

There are two things here of interest. One is the reported separation of the "pals" graves from that of Billy, on opposite sides of the little cemetery. Either the original reporter made a mistake about

The "Pals" monument, Fort Sumner, New Mexico.

Text of "Pals" monument.

the unmarked placement of Bowdre and O'Folliard or the popular twentieth century belief that they and Billy were buried side by side is in error.

The second point of interest in the *Optic* story is appearance of the first firm reference to Billy's grave marker, "a plain board with stenciled letters." How long it lasted is uncertain, but by 1884 it had been stolen or shot to pieces by vandals.

In that year a young cattleman Jack Potter had come to work for the New England Livestock Company which was acquiring government land surrounding Fort Sumner. Although Billy had been dead for three years, Potter found that he was still the main topic of conversation in those parts along the Pecos. Not until 1930 did Jack Potter begin writing down his recollections of what he had heard concerning the Kid's death.

On the subject of a grave marker, he said this: "The day after the Kid's funeral, Pete Maxwell had his man pull a four-foot wooden picket from the parade ground fence (in front of the Maxwell house), saw off a foot or so, and nail it in a cross bar to the larger piece. It looked more like a T than a cross. On the bar was the inscription, "Billy the Kid (Bonney)" with the death date "July 14, 1881." To that he adds: "Later, this marker was stolen by relic hunters and the second one, which replaced it, was also stolen."[12]

It is clear that the picket cross was not the same grave marker as the stenciled board described and illustrated by the *Optic* in January of 1882. Apparently, Potter was unaware of the existence of the latter and, therefore, believed that the picket cross he heard about had to be the original, when in reality it seems to have been the second marker, installed as a replacement.

In elaborating further, Jack Potter declares that the directors of the New England Livestock Co. had traveled out from the East on one occasion to inspect the Fort Sumner property. Finished and preparing to leave, they visited the old cemetery to see Billy the Kid's grave.

Potter went with them and recalled that the picket marker leaned at an angle because its base had rotted in the ground. As the directors were departing the cemetery, one of them named Chauncey said he was going to take Billy's cross back to Boston and put it in a museum.

He did have the marker when the directors boarded their Concord coach. In the early 1930s, Jack Potter, who by then had gained some modest fame, received a letter from the aged driver of that stagecoach. He confirmed that one of the passengers had the Kid's marker strapped to the outside of his suitcase.[13]

Among his recollections, Potter provides several details about Billy the Kid's funeral that differ from others' accounts. For instance, he claims that Vicente Otero's wood-hauling wagon, not merchant Manuel Abreu's delivery hack, was pressed into service as the horse-drawn hearse. Of more significance is his reference to the part played by Hugh Leeper, a Texas outlaw with a price on his head, but paradoxically also a Bible scholar.

The simple folk of Fort Sumner had nicknamed Leeper "The Sanctified Texan." In the words of Jack Potter, "He believed in predestination, preached the funeral, and said that Billy's time had certainly come at last." After extensive remarks at the graveside, which included relevant passages from the 14th chapter of Job, The Sanctified Texan proclaimed in conclusion: "Billy cannot come back to us, but we can go to him and will see him again up yonder. Amen."[14]

This version of the Kid's last rites strays widely from the tradition passed on by Hispanics: that Antonio Savedra simply led mourners in a prayer or two in Spanish, the language of the majority then of Fort Sumner residents. Savedra's familiar utterances would have been remembered by them, while Hugh Leeper's preaching, delivered in English, would not. That seems to offer the simplest possible explanation for the apparent discrepancy in the nature of Billy's funeral. That is, both Leeper and Savedra had their turn.

In the mid 1890s, the New England Livestock Co. had liquidated its cattle interests and piecemeal sold off the land within the vast Fort Sumner ranch. In the process, one of the owners, Lon Horn, tore down the old Maxwell house, where Billy the Kid breathed his last, salvaged the lumber and used it in the building of a ranch house thirty miles east on the Llano Estacado.

The vacant adobe buildings of the fort fell into ruin. Members of Lucien Maxwell's original colony, many of them friends of the Kid, were now dispersed. Some moved to new communities in the area, while others left the territory. Jack Potter in his old age paid a final visit to the site of the army fort and was unable to find any trace of it.[15]

By the end of the nineteenth century, the historic cemetery was without markers of any kind. Persons who had attended Billy's funeral, however, upon their own visits still confidently pointed to what they believed was the location of his grave. Their task became more difficult, however, after September 30, 1904.

On that date, according to Billy the Kid scholar Frederick Nolan, "The Pecos broke its banks and the entire area was flooded for a week to a depth of four feet...."[16] An earlier flood in the 1890s had taken out Fort Sumner's notorious Beaver Smith Saloon, situated 200 feet west of the officers quarters and close to the Pecos River. The larger inundation of 1904 claimed most of the now-vacant site of the Maxwell house, the ground there falling into the raging current. The spreading waters undermined the remaining military buildings and covered the cemetery.[17]

In the fall of 1905, twenty-five years after slaying the Kid, Pat Garrett guided western writer Emerson Hough of Chicago to the Fort Sumner cemetery. In his 1907 book, Hough described what they found.

"We entered the little barb wire enclosure of... . this wind swept and forgotten graveyard. There are no headstones.... Even the headboard which once stood at the Kid's grave—and which was once riddled with bullets by cowards who would not have dared to shoot that close to him had he been alive—was gone."

Pat Garrett, after the passage of so many years, had to make a search in the salt grass and greasewood. But at last, he declared: "Here is the place. We buried them all in a row. The first grave is the Kid's, and next to him is Bowdre and then O'Folliard." He and his posse had killed all three. Other sources say that the first grave holding the Kid was on the north end of the row.

In a reflective mood, Garrett returned to their buckboard where he picked up the canteen for a drink. Raising it in the manner of a toast, he said quietly: "Well, here's to the boys, anyway. If there is any other life, I hope they'll make better use of it than they did of the one I put them out of."[18]

As already mentioned, the earliest reference to the positioning of the three graves, cited by the Las Vegas *Daily Optic* just six months after Billy's interment has him on the opposite side of the small cemetery from Bowdre and O'Folliard. Was the paper's original statement wrong, or did Garrett's memory, after the elapse of a quarter century, fail him?

In 1896 an effort began on the part of the government to remove the burials of soldiers from cemeteries at abandoned forts scattered throughout New Mexico. Some of the remains were turned over to relatives elsewhere in the country, but the majority, among them many classified as "unknown soldiers," were sent to Santa Fe, the territorial capital then possessing the only national cemetery in the Southwest."[19]

Nolan reports that between January 1863 and February 1868, while Fort Sumner had an active garrison, twenty-two military burials were recorded. In 1906, less than two years after the great flood, he says that all the bodies in the military graves were disinterred and reburied at the Santa Fe National Cemetery. And he adds that "it is not entirely impossible that the Kid's remains were moved at the same time."[20] In fact, this writer some years ago heard Albuquerque journalist and author Howard Bryan say that Billy the Kid might very well have been inadvertently removed from Fort Sumner and placed in "an unknown soldier's grave" at Santa Fe.

That is not entirely implausible. Ex-cowboy Charles A. Siringo in his book *History of "Billy the Kid"* (1920), identifies Will E. Griffin as the man who moved all the bodies of the soldiers buried at Fort Sumner to the Santa Fe National Cemetery. His father was William W. Griffin, the U.S. government deputy surveyor and engineer who surveyed the whale-size Maxwell land grant, just prior to its sale. The son Will, who was listed as secretary of Santa Fe's Fairview Cemetery Company in 1895 and afterward was a member of Teddy Roosevelt's Rough Riders, probably carried out the disinterment and reburial under a government contract awarded to Charles W. Dudrow of Santa Fe.[21]

In 1999 Frederick Nolan published a brief article, "The Dudrow Map of 1906," which he cited simply as located in the National Archives among documents concerning sales of land from Lucien B. Maxwell's original purchase at Fort Sumner. A facsimile of the map is printed with the article.

It is a sketch map drawn to scale by Dudrow of the Fort Sumner military cemetery showing twenty-two soldiers' numbered graves. Burials of five children are concentrated in the northwest corner, three of them identified as "unknown."

The 28th numbered grave is that of Billy the Kid, while the 29th and 30th graves are south of his plot and shown on the map only as "Members of the Kid's Gang," with no names given. The 30th is considerably out of line to the east of the other two.

All of these graves lie in the western half of the cemetery. The eastern half contains civilian dead, mainly Maxwell employees. But recall that it was in this section that *The Daily Optic* in 1882 placed Bowdre and O'Folliard's graves.[22]

It is curious that Charlie Siringo, seeing Griffin in Santa Fe, quotes him as saying that "when the work was finished, the only graves left in the graveyard were those of Billy the Kid and his chum Tom O'Phalliard [O'Folliard]. On those two graves, close together, still remain the badly rotted wooden head boards." Oddly, Emerson Hough and Pat Garrett had found no headboards or other markers on their Fort Sumner visit just the year before. Did Griffin have reason to color the truth?[23]

If he was in possession of the Dudrow map during the project, he would have known the location of the Kid's and "the gang members'" graves and could have avoided disturbing them, even if there had been no head boards. He would also have been aware of the civilian burials in the east half of the cemetery.

Records show, however, that at this time forty-three sets of remains from Fort Sumner were received by the national cemetery at Santa Fe for reburial.[24] Since the Dudrow map demarcates twenty-two military graves, we have to assume that the twenty-one "extras", needed to make the figure of forty-three, probably came from the civilian half of the property. Griffin's statement that only Billy the Kid and O'Folliard were still in the graveyard would seem to support that conclusion. Future research may yet untangle this knotty problem.

Still, we have to ask whether the grave removal project was botched or even fraudulent, and in the process could Billy's bones have been uprooted and hauled off to Santa Fe? Siringo, referring back to the 1906 excavations at Fort Sumner observed that "since then the old cemetery has been turned into an alfalfa field and the chances are, all signs of this noted young outlaw's resting place have been obliterated."[25] So, does the Kid yet rest on the site of the Fort Sumner cemetery? The cloudy events of 1906, raise doubts, but otherwise leave us in the dark.

It ought to be pointed out, though, that Charlie Siringo firmly believed that Billy remained where his pallbearers had placed him in 1881. One day in the summer of 1916, as he relates it, he met a prominent woman of his acquaintance on the Santa Fe plaza, and she urged him to raise money to place a permanent monument on Billy the Kid's grave, "so that future generations would know where he was buried."

Adopting the idea, Siringo says, "I at once went to the monument establishment of Mr. Louis Napoleon and selected a fine marble monument, with the understanding that the inscription not be cut on it until after I had located the grave."

He concludes with this statement: "This is as far as the grave of Billy the Kid came to being marked, as the writer has been too busy on other matters to visit Fort Sumner and try to locate his last resting place." In fact, Charlie Siringo had ascertained that in some quarters there existed much "indignation at the idea of placing a monument at the grave of a blood thirsty outlaw." Such sentiment did not bode well for his initial hopes to collect contributions.

Within a short time, lingering negative attitudes toward the Kid would dissolve, and the public, which had almost forgotten his name, would suddenly embrace him as a stellar figure in the romantic Old West. The transformation in perspective began in 1926 when journalist Walter Noble Burns published his fictionalized *The Saga of Billy the Kid*. The quasi novel was a Book of the Month Club selection and became a bestseller. And suddenly Billy's fame had a new lease on life. Owing to Burns, he was brought back to national prominence, almost to the level of attention accorded him by the American press in 1881 upon the occasion of his untimely death.

A number of older New Mexicans who had lived through the Billy the Kid era expressed their displeasure with the Burns book, pointing out numerous errors of fact and historical misrepresentations. One of those critics was ex-territorial governor Miguel Antonio Otero, who in his youth had known the Kid briefly, and while acknowledging his faults, on the whole thought well off him.

Otero decided to begin assembling evidence on some of the controversial issues surrounding the Kid's history, particularly an old legend that Billy had not been slain by Pat Garrett but had escaped to Old Mexico and was still alive. In mid 1926 Otero's good friend, the adventurer Marshall Bond with his son Marshall, Jr., arrived in Santa Fe from California. When he learned of the governor's interest in Billy, Bond, Sr. proposed that Miguel and his wife join them on a tour of Lincoln County War sites and historic Fort Sumner. Governor Otero agreed and the little party departed Santa Fe by motor car on July 5. After various stops in Lincoln County, including an interview with an aging Susan McSween in the ghost town of

White Oaks, the group pressed on to Fort Sumner in De Baca County.

There Otero looked up Paulita Maxwell, Lucien's daughter, who was now Mrs. José Jaramillo. As he wrote afterward: "Despite the fact that Mrs. Jaramillo was suffering from rheumatism, she evinced a lively interest in the object of my visit and consented to drive with us to the old military cemetery in which Billy the Kid is buried."

The group found the small graveyard was still bounded by the barbed-wire fence mentioned by earlier visitors. Governor Otero refers to the soldiers' bodies having been exhumed and carried to Santa Fe's national cemetery. The remains of citizens, he declares, were left where they were, and maybe he was right. Yet, that seems at the very least questionable, given the government records cited above.

"Without hesitation," Otero continues, "Mrs. Jaramillo walked to a spot about twenty paces south of the old gateway, stopped, saying as she pointed directly in front of her: 'Here is where Billy the Kid is buried.'" That location does not readily correspond to the one described by *The Daily Optic* in 1882.

According to Governor Otero, Billy and two members of his band were buried in a row "in the order of their deaths—first Charlie Bowdre, then Tom O'Folliard, and finally Billy the Kid." (Actually, O'Folliard was killed first.) Like Pat Garrett in 1905, the governor in referring to the burials in a row fails to say on which end of the line the Kid had been placed.[26] Marshall Bond, Jr., writing long after their visit, confirmed that Billy's grave was still unmarked.[27]

While in the area, Otero and his party also met the Navajo servant Deluvina Maxwell, Jesús Silva, and Vicente Otero who provided their personal recollections of the Kid's slaying and his funeral. Not long afterward, Deluvina moved to Albuquerque and took up residence near today's Albuquerque High School. She died on November 27, 1927 without anyone having written down the story of her life.[28]

The year 1931 saw the next benchmark in the on-going history of the famous grave. In that year, a large stone block incised with the names of Tom O'Folliard, William H. Bonney, and Charlie Bowdre, including the death dates of each, was placed over their communal burial. A one-word heading at the top read simply, "Pals." This monument represents the first substantial effort to permanently mark the site.

Charles W. Foor (or "Uncle Charlie"), it is acknowledged, spearheaded the effort at raising funds to erect this tombstone. His attempts to interest government in assuming the expense failed, but by saving tips and donations received from tourists that he guided to the gravesite, the monument was acquired and installed.

At the time, it was said: "The exact location of the grave was never lost because Uncle Charley visited it daily from the day the Kid was buried until the marker was erected."[29] That rather preposterous statement probably originated with Foor himself who made other unverifiable claims, among them that he had been a friend of Billy the Kid and had served as one of his pallbearers.

On July 31, 1927, Uncle Charley filed at the De Baca County courthouse in the modern town of Fort Sumner his own hand-drawn colored map of the layout of the old fort as it looked in 1881. A marginal note, also in his hand, indicates that he became a resident of the fort in October of that year. The document with his signature is notarized by the De Baca County clerk. Thus, Foor was not on the scene until two and a half months after the shooting and interment of Billy the Kid.[30]

A news story in 1923 had reported that members of the State Highway Department visited old

Fort Sumner where they interviewed Charles Foor. He pointed out to them the exact location of the grave, which was a good twenty feet from the spot usually so identified. "Mr. Foor recalled many incidents out of the flaming past."[31]

With publication of Burns's *The Saga of Billy the Kid* in 1926, public interest in the desperado grew enormously, swelling the numbers of tourists annually visiting the grave. This book became the basis for noted Hollywood director King Vidor's MGM film "Billy the Kid" starring young Johnny Mack Brown in the title role. It was the first in a long line of motion pictures centered on the Kid's dramatic career.[32]

Some of the scenes were shot on location in the Fort Sumner area. Actor Brown, much taken with the character he was playing, donated $150 to Charlie Foor's monument fund. King Vidor also made a contribution. Earlier in 1930, the graduating class of Fort Sumner High School had taken as its senior project the covering of Billy the Kid's grave with a cement slab and the encircling of all three graves with a cement curb. Later, when the "Pals" monument was readied, local residents funded an elevated base for it and at the same time added slabs over the Bowdre and O'Folliard graves.[33]

Almost at once the monument came under the assault of souvenir hunters. "Chunks from fist size down to small pebbles have been knocked off the sides and top of the granite marker," lamented the *Fort Sumner Leader* on October 14, 1932. Unless a Society for the Prevention of Damage to Desperado Graves can be formed soon, it editorialized, the monument will have to be replaced within a year. Protection was soon provided by surrounding the grave-site with a nine foot high chain link fence.

Among the many new devoted fans of the Kid was James N. Warner of Salida, Colorado who had "read everything he could find about Billy." He also happened to be an accomplished stone cutter and proprictor of the Warner Memorial Service Co. Having become aware of complaints that the "Pals" monument was set over the middle grave and not directly over the Kid's end grave, Mr. Warner decided to produce and donate a smaller tombstone just for Billy. In this project he won the cooperation of the Fort Sumner Chamber of Commerce.

Warner selected and extracted a suitable piece of granite from his own quarry and in shop cut it to shape and added the chiseled inscription. On the gable or triangular cap appear the words "Truth and

History" above crossed pistols cut into the stone. Below them is a row of 21 chiseled bullets for the 21 men legend claims Billy killed.

On the main body of the tombstone's dark granite, large letters read: "Billy the Kid" followed by his supposed birth date of November 23, 1860 (sic) and the confirmed death date, July 14, 1881. At the bottom, visitors see: "The Boy Bandit King. He Died As He Had Lived."

Warner completed the stone dressing in March of 1940, and loading the tombstone and his daughter into the backseat of his car, he drove from Salida to Fort Sumner. At his destination, the stone was set inside the chain link fence over the space thought to contain the remains of Billy the Kid.[34]

For ten years the Warner stone was eagerly photographed by thousands of visitors, many of them probably believing that it was the original marker because of its "antique" look. Then in August 1950, it disappeared, stolen. Twenty-six years later, the missing tombstone turned up in Granbury, Texas southwest of Dallas. Joe Bowlin, a Fort Sumner museum operator, drove there, reclaimed the artifact, and brought it home. On June 19, 1976, a large crowd assembled to watch the re-installation of Warner's granite grave

The Warner tombstone of 1940.

stone, as it was shackled in iron and anchored in cement.[35]

Incredibly, Billy's marker was stolen again in early February 1981. This time widespread news coverage resulted in its recovery within days in Huntington Beach, California. Governor Bruce King sent the De Baca County Sheriff John McBride to escort the wayward stone back to New Mexico on a commercial airliner.[36]

Fort Sumner officials assisted by Jarvis Garrett, son of Pat Garrett, formally reset the tombstone in ceremonies on May 30, 1981. Today, it and the "Pals" monument remain secure inside a protective cage constructed of heavy metal bars. Tourists still flock to the site, along with dedicated buffs who keep alive the memory of Billy the Kid.

Placement of the Warner tombstone in front of the "Pals" monument. (Mike Pitel photograph)

As a postscript to this narrative, reference must be made to several modern attempts to exhume the graves of Billy and his two companions. In 1961 a relative of Charlie Bowdre claimed that his ancestor was not buried at Fort Sumner next to Billy the Kid, but rather on the George W. Coe ranch at Glencoe in Lincoln County. Coe was a staunch McSween supporter during the war and fought alongside his friends Charlie Bowdre and the Kid.

Coe's daughter clarified the matter by telling Alan Rhodes (son of New Mexico cowboy and author Eugene Manlove Rhodes) that her father, who died in 1941, had wanted to have all three bodies of the outlaws removed from Fort Sumner and reburied on the Coe ranch. But that proved impossible because he could not obtain proper authorization.[37]

In another case beginning in June of 1961, Miss Lois Telfer, a New York City beautician claiming to be a distant kinsman of Billy the Kid, petitioned the De Baca County district court for permission to remove his remains from Fort Sumner for reburial in Lincoln County. Her action created a storm, after the Lincoln county commission supported her effort.[38]

The following March 1962, Federal District Judge B. T. Hensley denied Miss Telfer's petition and dismissed the case. His ruling in part was based on the assumption that Billy the Kid's bones might no longer be in the Fort Sumner grave.

Subsequently, Telfer's claim to being the Kid's only living relative was discredited. Frederick Nolan described her, accurately it would seem, as "a self-styled descendant."[39]

In conclusion, for completeness on the subject of Billy the Kid's grave, one final bizarre episode extending over a year and a half has to be given at least passing attention. In early spring of 2003, the Lincoln County Sheriff Tom Sullivan launched a formal investigation into the now distant killings of deputies Bob Ollinger and James Bell at the hands of the Kid. For good measure, he proposed to re-examine controversial issues surrounding his predecessor Pat Garrett's slaying of Billy at Fort Sumner.

From the beginning, Sheriff Sullivan and several other county officials who supported his actions sought the exhumation of Billy's remains from Fort Sumner and those of his mother Catherine Antrim from the Memory Lane Cemetery at Silver City. Their hope was that comparing the DNA of the two might answer some of the lingering historical questions about the Kid's death and burial.[40] Prominent among those was the old speculation over whether Garrett had shot to death Billy the Kid, or someone else.

In June 2003, New Mexico Governor Bill Richardson called a news conference with Sheriff Sullivan in attendance. He announced appointment of a Santa Fe attorney to represent the interests of Billy the Kid in the forthcoming proceedings and hinted that if new information became available, he might consider a pardon for the outlaw. Richardson also made reference to the boost New Mexico tourism would receive through publicity the investigation would generate.[41]

As it unfolded, the issue causing the most controversy centered on opening of Billy's and Mrs. Antrim's graves. The two counties involved, De Baca and Grant, vigorously opposed any such disturbance. An obvious problem was that no one could guarantee bones unearthed from under the tombstones of either the mother or son would match the names on the stones. In September 2004, Sheriff Sullivan and his associates abruptly dropped their request to exhume bodies, an action that effectively ended the legal investigation and the flurry of media attention.[42] Jay Miller's book, *Billy the Kid Rides Again, Digging for the Truth* (Sunstone Press, 2005), gives a running account of the whole episode.

It has been said that Billy the Kid is the second most recognizable American name in the world, exceeded in fame only by Elvis. If that is so, it would explain why much of the planet, including *The New York Times*, German television, and the British Broadcasting Corporation seemed eager to follow the sometimes capricious twists and turnings of this on-going story. The episode served as another reminder that the Billy the Kid mystique still maintains a firm hold on the public imagination.[43]

In the final analysis, can any sort of answer be given to the original question: "Where is Billy buried?" Given the amount of conflicting data summarized in this account, it would seem that the mystery is unlikely ever to be solved. The present writer, however, believes it is most probable that Billy the Kid continues to "lie restless in his grave" in the Fort Sumner cemetery, somewhere in the vicinity of the two caged markers.

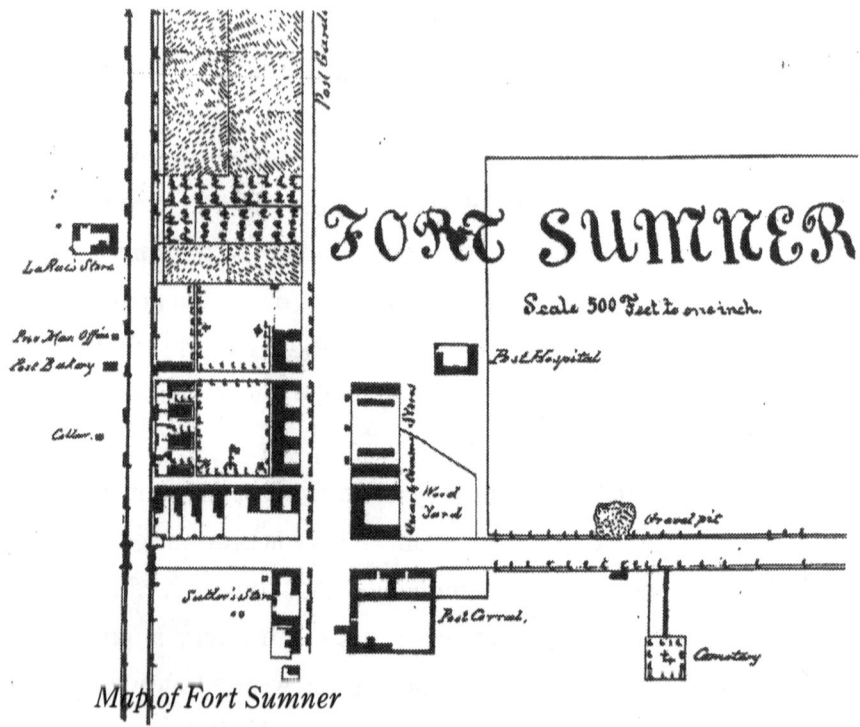

Map of Fort Sumner

APPENDIX 1

(The Rio Grande Republican (Las Cruces),
July 23, 1881)

SETTLERS REJOICE

The death of the young desperado known as "Billy the Kid," who succumbed to the fatal bullet of Sheriff Pat Garrett, of Lincoln county, on Friday night of last week, is the subject of great rejoicing throughout the entire territory and many are the persons who had incurred his displeasure who will rest much easier with him below than above the ground. Since he entered the killing business two years ago Kid has been a terror to honest, law-loving people and hence the general feeling of satisfaction at his decease, and deep-seated gratitude to the man who marked him for burial. Sheriff Garrett and his two assistants when they started for Fort Sumner in pursuance of this official duty took their lives into their hands. It was a death game they proposed to play, with the chance strictly even, but there was no shirking of the task nor flinching from the duty which Mr. Garrett felt rested upon him to accomplish this end.

It is not to be supposed that the paltry $500 reward offered for the Kid's life or capture could have been much of influence in instigating Sheriff Garrett to the deed of bravery and we are bound to give credit to his conscientious duty as an officer but yet it is not to be supposed that the reward offered nor any other substantial testimonial of gratitude will come amiss to him. The people certainly owe him much and nearly every town in the territory is moving to show a cash appreciation of its gratitude. All are equally interested and every place should come up with its mite. Mr. Garrett states that it is his intention to resign his office now that he has the burden of his duty off his hands. His retirement will be a loss to Lincoln county. He has, however, achieved a fame which will be undying and all will wish him all possible success in whatever new undertaking he may engage.

APPENDIX 2

Las Vegas Daily Optic
January 16, 1882

"THE BIVOUAC OF THE DEAD."

A Visit to an Old Burying Ground at Fort Sumner.

Special Correspondence of The Optic.

To the southwest of the abandoned and decaying Fort Sumner lies the graveyard, surrounded by what was once a good adobe wall, but from decay and neglect is now merely an outline, surrounding an acre of ground. We enter on the north, walking over the remains of the once handsome gate. To the left, in the northeast corner, are the graves of four rustlers—Grant, killed by Billy, the Kid; Ferris, who was killed by Barney Mason at the instance of the Kid, and O'Fallion and Bowdre, who were killed by Pat Garret and posse. These graves are all unmarked, and that of Bowdre shows the scratching of some hungry coyote, who seems to have been scared away by something before he reached his prey.

To the right of the entrance lies the grave of Billy the Kid, marked by a plain board, with the stenciled letters:

```
"BILLY
  THE
  KID"
```

It snowed last night, and the only marks on the grave were the tracks of a rabbit or skunk.

The southwest part of the little burying ground is filled with graves of soldiers who were killed in a fight with Indians near the fort as the few legible headboards read, "July 7, 1866."

Over in the southwest corner lies the grave of Lucien B. Maxwell, once so famous in New Mexico.

This "silent city of the dead" this morning, with the snow covering the graves, looks dreary, deserted and neglected, and we think, as we look at the white mounds, that the brave soldiers who fell fighting doing their duty, would spurn the company of the rustlers from their silent bivouac.

I. N. P.

APPENDIX 3

Pathfinder
In Search of Billy the Kid
New Mexico State Records Center and Archives
1205 Camino Carlos Rey
Santa Fe, New Mexico 87505

Compiled by Melisa Sanchez

SCOPE

The New Mexico State Records Center and Archives (SRCA) is a major source of information for any individual performing research on William H. Bonney, alias Billy the Kid. This pathfinder is designed to facilitate research and assist the patron in gathering core materials on Billy the Kid. The primary and secondary sources provided should contribute to the patron's ability to plan a more extensive project. All the material referred to in this pathfinder is located at the State Records and Archives; however, many of these same resources can be found in other libraries and archives.

INTRODUCTION

Despite his death in 1881, Billy the Kid has refused to take his place amongst the daisies. He is kept alive by researchers all around the world who are fascinated with this 19th century character. While numerous books, articles, and movies have been written and released, Billy the Kid scholars continue to search for new information on this well-known American outlaw. As a result, the Archives and Historical Services Division is at times inundated with correspondence, e-mails. faxes, and telephone calls, all requesting information on Billy the Kid. In response to this demand, this pathfinder was been created to assist patrons locate specific materials on Billy the Kid. A packet, including photocopies of the most requested items, is also available.

Before using the State Records Center and Archives, it is recommended that preliminary research be conducted first. Review as much secondary materials as possible. Once the preliminary research is compiled, the State Records Center and Archives has many resources to help continue your research. The sources listed in this pathfinder are intended to familiarize the beginning Billy the Kid researcher with the different types of primary material available at the SRCA.

OUTLINE

Primary Sources
- Territory of New Mexico vs. William Bonney, alias "Kid", alias William Antrim. Doña Ana County Criminal Case Nos. 531 and 532. (1878).
- Reward for the arrest of Billy the Kid, December 3, 1880. TANM, Roll 21, Frame 565.
- Lew Wallace authorization of $500 reward for the capture of William Bonney, December 13, 1880. TANM, Roll 99, Frame 172.
- Death warrant of Billy the Kid. Lincoln County, April 30. 1881 TANM. Roll 21. Frames 581 and 582.
- Attorney General's opinion regarding the reward payment due Pat Garrett for the death/capture of Billy the Kid. July 21, 1881. TANM, Roll 21, Frame 595.
- Copies of death warrant, Sheriff's certificate of Billy the Kid's escape and the jury's verdict verifying the death of Billy the Kid. Lincoln County Records. Box 2. Folder 132.
- Sheriff's request for payment for transporting Billy the Kid from Mesilla to Lincoln, 1881. TANM, Roll 47, Frame 335.
- Letter from Governor Sheldon to Legislature approving the payment of reward to Pat Garrett for the death of Billy the Kid, February 14, 1882. TANM, Roll 5, Frame 765; Roll 6, Frame 127; NM Law 1882, page 191.
- Certificate by Colonel Pennypacker that witnesses in Lincoln County War are not available to testify at the District Courts in Doña Ana and Socorro

Counties. May 19, 1879. Adjutant General Collection, Fort Stanton File.

Secondary Sources
- History File. Folder No. 20 contains articles, newspaper clippings, stories, and letters regarding Billy the Kid
- Donald Cline Collection

Websites
- www.thehistorynet.com/wildwest/articles/
- www.edd.state.nm.us/FACTBOOK/history.htm
- www.newmexico.org/culture/museums.html
- www.umkc.edu/imc/nmexico.htm
- www.britannica.com/seo/b/billy-the-kid/
- www.btkog@nmia.com
- www.zianet.com/snm/billykid.htm

Bibliography
- The Authentic Life of Billy, the Kid, By Pat F. Garrett, Norman: University of Oklahoma Press, 1954
- History of "Billy the Kid," By Chas. A. Siringo, 1920
- The Saga of Billy the Kid, By Walter Noble Bums, Doubleday, Page & Company, 1926
- The Tragic Days of Billy the Kid, By Frazier Hunt, Hastings House Publishers. New York. 1956
- The Death of Billy the Kid, By John W. Poe, Houghton Mifflin Company, 1933

APPENDIX 4

"BILLY QUOTES"

"The Lincoln County War proved nothing and established nothing. Practically everyone who shouldered arms ended up either dead or dead broke."
—Frederick Nolan

"Billy the Kid must remain wholly the most unaccountable figure in frontier history."
—Arthur Chapman

"He was a mere boy in appearance, always jovial and high-spirited; but in an emergency he always stood out as a leader, quick, resolute and firm."
—George L. Barber
(second husband of Susan McSween)

"Billy was a graceful and beautiful dancer, and when in the company of a woman he was at all times extremely polite and respectful."
—Governor Miguel A. Otero

"It is clear that Billy the Kid had gifts of leadership far in excess of the ordinary outlaw."
—Marshall Bond, Jr.

"A majority of the entire population [of Fort Sumner] were in sympathy with the Kid, while the remainder were in terror of him."
—Deputy U.S. Marshal John W. Poe

"The Kid ruled his gang with a rod of iron.... In spite of his discipline, however, his men fairly worshiped him and would have backed him with their lives any time it might become necessary."
—Dr. Henry F. Hoyt

"Actually, Billy the Kid was just a little, small-sized cow- and horse-thief who lived grubbily and missed legal hanging by only a few days."
—Jack Thorp

"I never knew a braver man than Billy. He did not know the meaning of fear."
—Ygenio Salazar

"Of the various bandits, renegades and outlaws of [the Wild West], Billy the Kid has been one of the most mythologized."
—John-Michael Rivera

"I have many times regretted that I had to kill him. I would have preferred taking Billy alive."
—Pat Garrett

"Billy died, not in a blaze of glory, but like a butchered yearling, shot down in the dead of night in his stocking feet...."
—Jack Thorp

"To this day no one knows just which grave is Billy's or where it lies...."
—Donald Cline

"The days of Billy the Kid are long since over, and one can scarcely realize that such a character ever lived among us."
—New Mexico Governor L. Bradford Prince, 1889

NOTES

BILLY THE KID'S MOTHER
[1] Much of what has been said thus far is arguable. For example, see Donald Cline, *Alias Billy the Kid* (1986), pp. 11-26.
[2] The Kid's life in Silver City is well covered in Jerry Weddle, *Antrim is My Stepfather's Name* (1993).

A FIRST JAIL BREAK
[1] Bob Alexander, *Single-Guns and Single-Jacks, A History of Silver City and Southwestern New Mexico* (2005), pp. 91-92.
[2] Philip J. Rasch, *Trailing Billy the Kid* (1995), pp. 48; 56.

THE KILLING OF JUAN PATRÒN
[1] Pat F. Garrett, *The Authentic Life of Billy the Kid* (annotated edition by Frederick Nolan, 2000), pp. 105-06.
[2] Miguel Antonio Otero, *The Real Billy the Kid* (1936), p. 114.

AN ENGLISHMAN MEETS BILLY
[1] Townshend's memory failed him. The man's name was Beckwith (Hugh).

SOME BILLY THE KID IMPOSTERS
[1] On Miller see Helen Airy, *Whatever Happened to Billy the Kid?* (1993). And for Roberts consult C. L. Sonnichsen and William V. Morrison, *Alias Billy the Kid* (1955); and. W. C. Jameson, *Billy the Kid, Beyond the Grave* (2005).
[2] Peña included a sketch of Max Miller in his *Memories of Cibola* (1997).

A GRAVE QUESTION: WHERE IS BILLY BURIED?

[1] Robert W. Frazer, *Forts of the West* (Norman: University of Oklahoma Press, 1965), p. 104; and, Lawrence R. Murphy, *Lucien Bonaparte Maxwell, Napoleon of the Southwest* (Norman: University of Oklahoma Press, 1983), p. 190.

[2] Murphy, *Maxwell*, p. 191.

[3] Murphy, *Maxwell*, p. 202.

[4] Donald Cline, *Alias Billy the Kid, The Man Behind the Legend* (Santa Fe, N.M.: Sunstone Press, 1986), p. 116. And, George Atwood,"Billy the Kid's Grave," *The Kid* (Zane Productions, Issue no. 2, Sept. 1989), p. 2.

[5] A.P "Paco" Anaya, *I Buried Billy* (College Station, Texas Creative Publishing Co., 1991), p. 131. And, Pat F. Garrett, *The Authentic Life of Billy the Kid* (Annotated edition by Frederick Nolan; Norman: University of Oklahoma Press, 2000), p. 178.

[6] Miguel Antonio Otero, *The Real Billy the Kid* (New York: Rufus Rockwell Wilson, Inc., 1936), pp. 156; 158. And, Anaya, *I Buried Billy*, p. 132. As coffin material, Silva used boards salvaged from the roof of an abandoned adobe building. The obituary of Vicente Otero in the *El Paso Times*, Feb. 7, 1935 stated that "he was reputed to have dug the grave of Billy the Kid." Walter Noble Burns in his "novel" *The Saga of Billy the Kid* (New York: Doubleday, Page & Co., 1926) declares that handy man Domingo Lubacher knocked together Billy's coffin, while ranch employee Francisco Medina dug his grave. A few authors have accepted his identification as valid. See e.g., Marion Ballert, *Billy the Kid, A Date With Destiny* (Seattle: Superior Publishing Co., 1970), p. 119.

[7] Bill Rakocy, *Billy the Kid* (El Paso: Bravo Press, 1985), p. 235.

[8] Rasch, *Trailing Billy the Kid* (n.p.: National Ass'n. for Outlaw and Lawman History, Inc., 1995), p. 139.

[9] Billy's trigger finger was later reported to have been placed on exhibit at county fairs in Indiana.

[10] Garrett, *The Authentic Life* (2000 ed.), p. 178.

[11] A facsimile of this article, entitled "The Bivouac of the Dead" appears hereinafter as Appendix 2. And, Anaya, *I Buried Billy*, p. 150.

[12] In print, Potter's remarks on the grave marker are available in two different places, with some small variance in detail: Jean M. Burroughs, *On the Trail, The Life and Tales of "Lead Steer"* Potter (Santa Fe, N.M.: Museum of New Mexico Press, 1980), p. 139; and, "Billy the Kid Grave Marker" in the *El Paso Herald-Post*, May 19, 1934, based upon a letter to the paper from Potter, who was then a member of the House of Representatives in the New Mexico State Legislature.

[13] *El Paso Herald-Post*, May 19, 1934. Article reprinted in Rakocy, *Billy the Kid*, p. 262.

[14] Burroughs, *On the Trail*, pp. 105; 138-39.

[15] Burroughs, *On the Trail*, pp. 31-32.

[16] Nolan, *The West of Billy the Kid* (Norman: University of Oklahoma Press, 1998), p. 288.

[17] Burroughs, *On the Trail*, pp. 32; 106.

[18] Emerson Hough, *The Story of the Outlaw* (New York: Grosset & Dunlap, 1905), p. 311. Leon Metz dwells on Garrett's return to the grave in his *Pat Garrett, The Story of a Western Lawman* (Norman: University of Oklahoma Press, 1973), p. 126.

[19] Santa Fe *Daily New Mexican*, June 19, 1897.

[20] Nolan *The West of Bill the Kid* p. 288.

[21] Siringo, *History of "Billy the Kid"* (reprint ed.; Austin: Steck-Vaughn Co., 1967), pp. 138-39. And, Murphy, *Lucien Maxwell*, pp. 174; 182. The exact business relationship of Griffin and Dudrow is not clear. On Siringo's association with Billy the Kid in the Texas Panhandle, see Howard R. Lamar, *Charlie Siringo's West* (Albuquerque: University of New Mexico Press, 2005), pp. 81-83.

[22] Frederick W. Nolan, "The Dudrow Map of 1906," *The Outlaw Gazette*, 12 (Nov 9 1999), pp. 8-9. The map was drawn on a sheet containing Charles Dudrow's letterhead, which revealed that he dealt in timber, coal, transfer and

storage. His moving capacity allowed by the transfer end of his business may have qualified him for the contract.

[23]Siringo, *History of "Billy the Kid,"* p. 139.

[24]Compiled Adjutant General's notes, National Cemetery Folder, History Verticle Files, New Mexico State Records Center and Archives, Santa Fe.

[25]For all of the Siringo quotes above see his *History of "Billy the Kid,"* pp. 137-40.

[26]For this quote and those immediately above, see Miguel Antonio Otero, *The Real Billy the Kid* (New York: Rufus Rockwell Wilson, Inc., 1936), pp. 110-11; 152.

[27]Marshall Bond, Jr., *Gold Hunter, The Adventures of Marshall Bond* (Albuquerque: University of New Mexico Press, 1969), p. 76.

[28]Rasch, *Trailing Billy the Kid*, p. 139. And, Rose P. White, "Full Many a Flower ... The Story of Deluvina," *The Outlaw Gazette* 13 (Nov. 2000), pp, 24-25.

[29]George Shumard, *Billy the Kid, The Robin Hood of Lincoln County* (revised ed.; Deming, N.M.: Cambray Enterprises, 1976), p. 59.

[30]Shumard, *Billy the Kid*, pp. 49; 59. An undated photograph, p. 48, titled "Pallbearers," shows Vicente Otero, Charles Foor, Paco Anaya, and José Silva posing together, apparently in the dirt street of Lake Valley, a southern New Mexico ghost mining town. It is an odd image, especially if it is authentic. An outline version of Foor's Fort Sumner map is printed in Anaya, *I Buried Billy*, pp. 130-31. Walter Noble Burns at the end of his *The Saga of Billy the Kid* has a chapter describing his own visit to the Fort Sumner cemetery in the mid 1920s with Charlie Foor serving as his guide. A short biography of Kentucky-born Foor appears in *The Outlaw Gazette* 12 (Nov. 1999), p. 3

[31]Santa Fe *New Mexican*, June 28, 1923. Rakocy, *Billy the Kid*, p. 199.

[32]Jon Tuska, *Billy the Kid, A Handbook* (Lincoln: University of Nebraska Press, 1983), pp. 163-65.

[33]*Fort Sumner Leader*, Oct. 31, 1930. And, interview

with Don Sweet of Fort Sumner, Jan. 24, 2006. The monument was ordered in October 1930, but was probably not delivered and installed until the following year.

[34]*El Paso Times*, April 10, 1940. *Albuquerque Journal*, June 3, 1976. Note that on May 29, 1949, a memorial stone with text and map honoring Lucien Maxwell was placed a short distance from Billy's grave. Among dignitaries attending the formal ceremony were the governors of New Mexico and Colorado and the president of the Santa Fe Railroad. *Clovis News Journal*, May 31, 1949.

[35]*Albuquerque Journal*, June 20, 1976.

[36]*De Baca County News*, February 5; 17; and 19, 1981. An anonymous tip led to the arrest of a 25-year-old truck driver, Walter Nicolson, of Huntington Beach. He was charged with burglary and larceny in connection with the theft of the Kid's tombstone.

[37]Bill Kelly, "Bowdre Mystery Yet to be Laid to Rest," *New Mexico Magazine*, 71 (Feb. 1993), p. 34.

[38]*El Paso Herald-Post*, June 27, 1961 and March 13, 1962. Rakocy, *Billy the Kid*, p. 161.

[39]Nolan, *The West of Billy the Kid*, p. 4.

[40]Jan Girand, "The Battle for Billy's Bones, 2003-2004 Events Timeline," *The Outlaw Gazette* (2004/2005), pp. 2-6.

[41]*Albuquerque Journal*, Nov. 19, 2003.

[42]*Santa Fe New Mexican*, Sept. 25, 2004. For the problems associated with Catherine Antrim's burial (misspelled Katherine on her stone), see Jerry Weddle, *Antrim is My Stepfather's Name* (Tucson: Arizona Historical Society, 1993), pp. 55-56.

[43]For the full story of Sheriff Sullivan's "crusade;" consult Jay Miller, *Billy the Kid Rides Again* (Santa Fe: Sunstone Press, 2005).

SELECTED READINGS

The bibliographer and western writer Jeff C. Dykes in 1952 published a basic reference tool, *Billy the Kid, The Bibliography of a Legend* (University of New Mexico Press). It listed and described 437 books and articles plus a few songs and plays. In the second half of the 20th century, Dykes struggled to get a handle on the steady torrent of new Billy publications, so that he could update and re-issue his inventory. Upon his death in his eighties, the task was still incomplete.

Here I take note of a handful of books that have appeared in recent years, ones that I believe are especially significant and reliable.

A good place to start is with general histories of the Lincoln County War, which provide background for deeper studies of Billy the Kid. Pioneer works in this category are William A. Keleher, *Violence in Lincoln County, 1869–1881* (Albuquerque: University of New Mexico Press, 1957); and Robert N. Mullin, ed., *Maurice G. Fulton's History of the Lincoln County War* (Tucson: University of Arizona Press, 1968).

Renowned author Robert M. Utley wrote *High Noon in Lincoln, Violence on the Western Frontier* (Albuquerque: University of New Mexico Press, 1987), giving an overview of the conflict, which he described as "a war without heroes." At the same time, one of New Mexico's leading historians John P. Wilson gave us a book of broader scope with his *Merchants, Guns and Money, The Story of Lincoln County and Its Wars* (Santa Fe: Museum of New Mexico Press, 1987). While he focuses on the war, the text encompasses the full sweep of the county's raucous history.

For a denser treatment, readers can see Frederick Nolan, *The Lincoln County War, A Documentary History* (Norman: University of Oklahoma Press, 1992). Quoting broadly from statements by war participants, the book also presents a detailed chronological chart and a useful series of mini-biographies of key persons who played a role in the narrative.

Among biographies of Billy the Kid, I judge these to be the most useful and readable. Pat F. Garrett's *The Authentic Life of Billy the Kid*, first published in April 1882 and containing much fiction, has gone through several editions. The latest and most helpful is the one released by the University of Oklahoma Press in 2000, its chief merit residing in the commentary and extensive marginal annotations by Frederick Nolan.

Nolan's *The West of Billy the Kid* (Norman: University of Oklahoma Press, 1998) qualifies as a solid biography although the publisher touts it also as "a comprehensive photo gallery" that shows people and places that the Kid knew.

Not to be overlooked is Joel Jacobsen, *Such Men as Billy the Kid, The Lincoln County War Reconsidered* (Lincoln: University of Nebraska Press, 1994). The author, formerly an assistant attorney general for the State of New Mexico, explores for the first time the legal aspects of the war. His conclusions on a number of important matters are surprising.

The best introductory biography for a general audience is Robert M. Utley, *Billy the Kid, A Short and Violent Life* (Lincoln: University of Nebraska Press, 1989). Pulitzer Prize winner Larry McMurtry thinks it is "as definitive as anything we are likely to get on the brief life of Billy the Kid."

For those eager to plow deeper into the field of "Billy books," I can recommend a few additional titles. Jon Tuska's *Billy the Kid, A Handbook* (reprinted.; Lincoln: University of Nebraska Press, 1986) is a concise bio-bibliography which also tells at length how historians, fiction writers, and film makers have used and exploited the Kid's name. Also in that vein is Stephen Tatum, *Billy the Kid, Visions of the Outlaw in America, 1881-1981* (Albuquerque; University of New Mexico Press, 1982).

For many years Philip J. Rasch wrote short articles about Billy the Kid and those persons linked to his history. Unfortunately he did not live to see them collected and published in three volumes by the National Association for Outlaws and Lawmen in conjunction with the University of Wyoming, Laramie. The Rasch titles are *Trailing Billy the Kid* (1995); *Gunsmoke in Lincoln County* (1997); and *Warriors of Lincoln County* (1998). Each book is a goldmine of information.

I should also mention Harold L. Edwards, *Goodbye Billy the Kid* (College Station, Texas: Creative Publishing Co., 1995). Its pages contain a wide selection of Billy the Kid obituaries that appeared throughout the nation on the heels of his slaying. Sprinkled through them are informative nuggets, not to be missed.

Alias Billy the Kid, The Man Behind the Legend by Donald Cline (Sunstone Press, 1986) nicely balances the legend for both scholars and lay readers and has many historical photographs.

Helen Airy's *Whatever Happened to Billy the Kid*

(Sunstone Press, 1993) presents a highly controversial take on who might have been the "real Billy" (she points to John Miller) and was listed as suggested reading on a television documentary. Also interesting is *Billy the Kid, The Legend of El Chivato* by Elizabeth Fackler (Sunstone Press, 2003), critically acclaimed by *Publishers Weekly* and *Kirkus Reviews*.

And last, *Billy the Kid Rides Again, Digging for the Truth* by Jay Miller (Sunstone Press, 2005). It details how three sheriffs set out (in 2003) to prove that Pat Garrett killed Billy the Kid, thereby also proving that Brushy Bill of Hico, Texas was not the real Kid.

ABOUT THE AUTHOR

Photograph by Wally Anderson, 1961

Marc Simmons is a professional author and historian who has published more than forty books on New Mexico and the American Southwest.

His popular "Trail Dust" column is syndicated in several regional newspapers.

In 1993, King Juan Carlos of Spain admitted him to the knightly Order of Isabel la Católica for his contributions to Spanish colonial history.

ABOUT THE ILLUSTRATOR

Photograph by Ron Dewitt

Ronald Kil is an award winning Western artist and New Mexico working cowboy. He has illustrated dozens of books and magazines including this, his tenth book for Marc Simmons.
Ronald lives south of Santa Fe, New Mexico with his daughter Corrina, and his dog Reata.

ABOUT THE TYPE

This book was set in Century Old Style type.
The chapter headings in Algerian type.

www.ingramcontent.com/pod-product-compliance
Lightning Source LLC
Chambersburg PA
CBHW030140170426
43199CB00008B/137